Foal and the Angels

. . . .

Wisdom Comes Through:
A Journey of Understanding

Foal and the Angels

....

Wisdom Comes Through:
A Journey of Understanding

FOAL

TURNING
STONE
PRESS

First published in 2012 by
Turning Stone Press, an imprint of
Red Wheel/Weiser, LLC
With offices at:
665 Third Street, Suite 400
San Francisco, CA 94107
www.redwheelweiser.com

ISBN (paperback): 978-1-61852-022-7
ISBN (hardcover): 978-1-61852-021-0

Cover design by Jim Warner
Cover photograph © Elena Ray/Shutterstock.com

Printed in the United States of America
IBT
10 9 8 7 6 5 4 3 2 1

Contents

Introduction xi

The Beginning of All 1
The Angel of Compassion 5
The God-Horse Dream 8
The Angel of Now 12
Metatron 14
The Inner Child 17
The Caterpillar-Kids Dream 19
Archangel Mika-el 22
God Supreme 25
The Baggage Dream 26
The Christ 29
Archangel Mika-el 34
Lord Michael 36
Little Dot Dream 39
God Supreme 44
Angel EM 48
The Body-Suit Dream 51
Archangel Chamuel 56
The Demon Dream 59
The Souls' Race 67
God Supreme 69
Lord Michael 71

Archangel Chamuel 75
Archangel Gabriel 78
Lord Michael 80
The Stag Dream 82
The Golden Cobra Dream 84
Divine Mother 87
The Stick Dream 90
God Supreme 91
Angel EM 97
God Supreme 100
The "Kiddo" Dream 105

Epilogue 111

Dedicated to God

Lord, make me write this as
You want me to write it.

Acknowledgments

My most heartfelt thanks, filled with the deepest gratitude, to my trust-full friend, Patti Garver, who was the first ever to read this and, in spite of the busiest schedule, found the time to make the very first corrections. Patti, thank you for believing in Foal from the first!

Thanks also to Andy Boerger, who, with great insight, gave me invaluable suggestions, helped me link the various parts together, and drew such beautiful pictures. Thank you, dear friend! And to Michelle Karen, who saw this little book in the stars, already manifested, so many years ago. Thanks Michelle, your friendship is invaluable to me!

I am also deeply blessed to have received the support of Susan Buckley of the Messengers of Change group. Susan, I can't tell you enough how much I appreciate all you have been doing for me and all the care and love that I always feel when I talk with you. And to Marcelle Charrois, who edited the very first pages. Marcelle, you will be surprised to see it in this longer form, and I hope you still like it.

But to one person in particular I owe possibly the greatest thanks, and this is Julian Kalmar of Ten Million Clicks for Peace, because he was the one to tell me to make a book out of the first tentative pages. It is thanks to him and his wise counsel that *Foal and the Angels* came to life in the form that it is today. Thank you, Julian, for your great wisdom and insight.

And a very special "Thank you!" to Gary Bonnell, "my psychic," for being willing to take the time to actually read through the first script. I am so grateful for that, Gary! And to Jamie Butler for foreseeing a four-book series. Both of you are such rare jewels! Also I would especially like to thank Henry Reed of A.R.E. for showing me how to connect with my dreams. I am so very grateful for your teachings, Henry !

And then how could I not thank Ronna Hermann for writing the inspiring book that started me on this journey? *On Wings of Light* was indeed my wake-up call. Thank you, Ronna! I owe you big time!

And furthermore, I need to acknowledge all the help I received from invisible friends all along. I consider only about one tenth of this book mine. The rest was truly given to me and whispered into my mind by these beautiful Beings. And among them, one in particular offered the greatest assistance—a very special Being who helped with so much inspiration and the greatest love.

And last but not least, to my family, who sometimes had to put up with my not being totally available to them, and never, or rarely ☺, complained.

I thank you all with the greatest gratitude.

Introduction

I consider and have always considered myself to be a very well-balanced, totally grounded person, leading a very normal life.

I was born in a Western European country and studied several languages in order to become a simultaneous interpreter. My father was a doctor, and despite the fact that he was the best person in the whole world, he never talked of God or spiritual things. In my family I was the only one who went to church, maybe because I always felt this profound love for God inside. Nevertheless, I was always sitting alone in a dark corner of a small chapel inside the church, rather than taking an active part in the service.

Then, when I was 21, a very special thing happened. I was invited to a Tibetan meditation by a friend, and I remember being very nervous about it. It was a first for me. I had never meditated before in my life, but I was interested in Oriental cultures, and so I joined the meditation. The most vivid memory I have of this event is that as the Lama was approaching each of us with some sacred objects in his hand, all I could think of was that he would immediately know that my mind was all over the place and was doing anything but meditating. So when it was my turn, I was really ashamed of my unmanageable thoughts and got mentally ready for a scolding.

What happened next defies logic or any rational explanation. As the Lama touched my forehead with some kind of relic, the world disappeared. I had this great sense of Light, like successive waves of Light coming out, rising out of me, out of my belly, and reaching out and out and out. It happened. Like that. Unexpected, not even asked for, since I had no idea what to expect or ask for.

After this I found I was changed; so poised, so balanced, so perfect. And I just could not get angry. Try as I might, even in provoking situations that would have usually strongly irritated me, anger was nowhere to be found, it just could not rise. I clearly remember myself thinking "Oh, my God! I will never be able to get angry again!" I was in blissful synch for a few weeks. Then it faded away, but it left a deep mark within me. To this day, I still don't know why it happened so spontaneously.

The moment of short but intense momentary enlightenment in Foal's story gives a detailed picture of how it felt to me. It left me stunned and dazed, forced to believe the unbelievable.

While I received all the messages and dreams described here between 2004 and 2010, this experience actually goes back to 1975. And this is actually one of the very few liberties I took.

Then, just a bare month after this incredible thing happened, I met my Asian husband-to-be; I quickly and overwhelmingly fell in love, got married, and settled down in a foreign country. Adjusting to an Asian culture so totally different from mine absorbed the whole of me and took all my energy and time. I was preoccupied with being a good partner to my husband, raising kids, and working, all while learning a completely new language, culture, and cuisine, so that for almost 30 years, spiritual matters were left at the back of my mind, simmering there, relegated to a tiny corner in my brain.

Before going on with my story, let me stress this. I was so **not** a New Age person. I can't stress this enough. New Age was just not my thing. I had actually never even heard of the term New Age until, about 10 years ago, I found it in a book I was reading, but it was used in such unflattering tones that, from the very start, I was totally biased against it.

Well, as it goes, one Christmas, just before I turned 50, one of my daughters presented me with a New Age book, *On Wings of Light*, channeled by Ronna Hermann. I still remember so clearly that the only reason I started reading it was that I was worried that my daughter might have gotten into a cult, and I wanted to check it out. Well, talk about spirituality! In fact, this wonderful book proved to be a true revelation to me and changed my life in more ways than I could have imagined. More than the words themselves, it is what happened while I was reading through it that was a true "wake-up call" for me. As I was reading a certain passage, the words, "I am Archangel Michael," clearly stood out, totally overwhelming me.

I don't know how to explain this, but while my eyes fell on those words, it felt as if a huge presence had just landed in front of me and physically struck me on the chest so strongly that I felt like falling back a few feet. And in my mind I heard a voice saying **Hey!** *It is Me! Wake up! Don't you remember?*

I was shaken to the core. This was so incredibly real to me that I struggled for a rational explanation for several days. To me, this was not one of those things that I could share easily, at least not in my world, so I kept it close inside. And as I struggled to come to terms with it, the stunning dreams started and the out-of-body experiences, too. What's more, there was this feeling I could not shrug off of Essences all around me trying to communicate something to me. As I realized that all these incidents must be connected somehow, I came to see that moment with Archangel Michael as a true Clarion call.

All this happened almost at the same time, raising a thousand questions inside me and a desire to know more, to understand more. I naturally fell into this pattern of daily prayer and nightly meditation that started me on this journey of self-discovery. I received all the messages (and there are so many more, actually) in this book during meditation or just before falling asleep at night. The words would flow so fast in my mind, that often, to keep up with that pace, I had to skip a word or two, if not part of the sentence itself.

What I describe here is almost exactly how it happened, or at least, how it was felt and registered by my mind and in my mind. The main liberties I took were to squeeze the six-year span into a story that lasted just a few weeks and to leave out some repetitions. As for the dreams, I have reported them all exactly as they were. I have tried to keep as close to reality, to my reality, as I can.

So, is all this true? I don't know. How could anyone possibly know? But genuine? Yes. It totally comes from the heart. The fine line between my imagination and inspiration was unknowingly blurred into one of a bigger Truth, becoming a sort of thick pipeline between two different worlds. I experienced this from the inside out, living the fascinating and captivating dreams, being amazed at the beauty and wisdom of the messages. Nothing could be truer to me than this experience; nothing could be more real to me. It was an intensive course of wisdom, imparted through dreams, messages, and voices. I called it Angels' School.

It took me a long time to get over my ever-present self-questioning doubts. And now, at last, I have finally set it down into words—words that feel so inadequate, wanting, and imperfect to describe such an experience. But if the angels' messages and Foal's experiences can help people understand their lives better, I will find value in it, and it will all be so worth my efforts. And I wanted so much to share it anyway; it is just too beautiful to keep it all to myself.

Besides, I was asked to write this down. And God does not take no for an answer. My greatest hope is that this may be read and cherished not only by already spiritually connected persons, but also by the "layman," and that this may be the beginning of an awakening for them too, as it was for me.

This is a fairytale, a true fairytale.

It is about Foal and the angels.

☙ The Beginning of All ❧

Foal was looking up at the night sky again, feeling the same sense of awe and mystery that had allured him since he was a little child. The sense of peace, of silence, of distant unknowns that he could feel in the night sky had always been a balm to his heart. This feeling created a place, an imaginary place maybe, but a safe place to run away and hide from the bustle and hustle of everyday life. It was a safe place to pray to God, to seek God, to feel God closest to him.

Foal had always felt God as a nearby Presence, and more often than not, he would find himself explaining things to this Presence, just saying any kind of silly thing that might cross his mind. Foal, for no particular reason, was also convinced he knew what his life's purpose was. You see, in this lifetime, he was utterly determined to find God—not through pain and suffering, as he felt he had in so many lives before, but through joy, love, and happiness. And he was on a real mission to prove this to himself and to the world. "Watch me!" he thought. "No matter what, I am going to make it this time!"

This was his life—to succeed. He knew it. Nevertheless, despite all his fervor and resolution, he had the feeling that something was missing; there was something he needed to learn before he could really awaken to the life that he believed was his to live.

So he prayed and prayed and asked again and again for guidance. He knew somewhere, somehow, he was being heard, but he wondered why he could never quite get a clear answer.

Foal absolutely believed he was not alone and that there were so many essences of Beings, feelings of Beings around him, possibly angels who were trying to reach out to him. Signs of this were all around him—those whispers in his head, those waves of uncontrollable emotions, the inexplicable joy that sprang up from his heart for no reason at all. It just wasn't possible that he was alone. There had to be something, there—there just had to. He wanted so much to communicate, to ask what it was they wanted so much to say.

Yet he didn't know how to make the whispers in his head become words. So, Foal decided to start a game. He wrote names of angels on paper, his "Angels Map" as he called it, and he chose a crystal from among his many beautiful stones. Every night before he went to sleep, he would go deep into prayer; he would close his eyes and ask, "Who wants to talk to me the most tonight?" Then he would gently toss the crystal onto his Angel Map and see on whose name it had fallen. He would wait and keep quiet, listening for the silence to break, waiting for the whispers to turn into words. It was not easy. The first messages did not come right away. Foal doubted himself and feared he would not be able to hear anything; and if a message finally did come, he was worried that it might be from his imagination.

And then one night it happened. A Voice boomed in, seemingly coming from Foal's heart:

I AM God Supreme. I want to talk to you.

The Voice felt big and Foal felt very small, yet he was wary. He had never heard God called in such a way before. Supreme? Umm . . . what if it was not God? What if he was just dreaming? Hesitantly, he asked, "Are you really God? My God, the God of Love?"

The Voice laughed back, amused, *What, Foal? Do you require an ID with My picture on it? Don't you have faith in Me? Don't you love Me with all your heart?*

Foal was overwhelmed and he stuttered, "Sure, sure . . . . Sorry, um, God Supreme. I just wanted to make sure."

How many "sures" do you need, Foal? Tell Me, why are you so unsure? Where is the love and faith you always professed? If you can't have faith in yourself now, how can you have faith in Me? If you don't trust what you feel, how can you trust Me then?

Foal was dumbfounded. God was finally talking to him and he didn't know what to say or how to answer. Embarrassed to the extreme, he murmured, "Lord, I truly do not know anything, but I do know I am here speaking to You in this moment, in this place." Foal felt a beam of Light in his heart. The Beam went on speaking.

*That **IS** a good answer, Foal; that's all that counts, you see, that's all there is.* And then, quite abruptly, God asked, *Tell me then, are you willing?*

Foal blurted out, "Yes, of course I am willing. Umm . . . what is it exactly you want me to be willing for?"

*Foal? Are you **willing**?*

Foal was confused, but he couldn't possibly make God Supreme wait.

*Foal, **are you willing**?*

"Yes, Lord, I am."

Good, then let the angels come and speak their words to you.

~

And so it began. Each night, for many nights, the angels came. The first angel felt beautiful, feminine, and full of grace. Foal couldn't see her, but he could feel her, and finally, after some time, he could hear her. He felt her sweet voice all through his head. She called herself the Angel of Compassion, and she spoke in a soft, melodious voice.

☙ The Angel of Compassion ☙

Foal, heed what is being said. Come to the Love spot in your heart, where your Soul breathes. Where God is there for you and you are there for God, and Divinity becomes One again.

I bring you a message of compassion: compassion for the family and friends around you, for those not around you, for the people who must suffer and for the people who make others suffer, for the whole world.

Open your heart to needs untold.

Open your Soul to demands of Love.

Open your higher self to yourself.

The compassion you have, let it flow, and let it flow close, before it goes far.

Bleeding compassion springs forth to another Being.

The blood is the seed.

The bleeding heart sows beautiful seeds in the land.

Its vibration reaches down, density lifts up.

A bleeding heart is not all about suffering.

A bleeding heart bears the Child of Compassion.

From those blood drops, flowers spring and quench their thirst.

Do not be afraid of pain. It is only a façade.

It is not pain. It is a facet of Love, the Love of God.

A good life is not free of pain and worries.
A good life is full of these and their solutions.
In the finding of the solutions, you find your evolution.

Astonishing is the power of Love and the Light it sheds on the people it touches.
Cherish others for the wonderful Beings of Light they are.
See them with your shining eyes for the Light they hold inside.
Respect the Being of Light hidden in that clothing of flesh,
So you can mirror your Light, one into the other, and know.

Do not let yourself see yourself as you are, because you are not.
You are not what you see.
Human perception will see the human you.
Divine perception sees the Divine you.
This is how God sees you.
This is how God trusts you.
This is how God put faith in you and gave you life.

Life is a deed of trust.
God trusted you with life, Foal.
You were born because you were trusted.

Thus answer that trust and trust the Love of God that makes you move, that makes you think and feel. And rejoice in that trust, in that Love.
Feel the Love in the form of joy, rejoice in the joy.
And she was gone. Foal was pretty much speechless. His mind was spinning with the words inside of him. Wow, "You were born because you were trusted." Foal couldn't get these words out of his mind. God had trusted

him with life, what an overwhelming concept; he wanted to give back to that trust. How could he repay such trust?

"How can I give back to You, Lord? How can I feel Your joy in my being more and more? I want to channel such joy. I am trustful and grateful for such joy. Let me be the channel of Your joy."

The booming Voice spoke to him again, and Foal felt like falling into a cocoon of Love, pure Love, almost hot in its essence.

Through all your pores you can breathe Me in, Foal.

Whatever part of Me you want to channel is yours.

Be the channel of My grace, of your grace.

My joy already resides in your cells.

My joy is your very being.

My joy is in the blood, in your veins.

My joy is in the life of you.

Love your body.

See Me there before you see Me anywhere else.

Oh, the Love and joy Foal felt in that moment, there were no words to describe. He felt warm and cocooned all over. He basked in that warmth the whole night. And Foal had a dream that night—the most beautiful dream.

⮞ The God-Horse Dream ⮜

In the dream, Foal was a young boy and was watching two men walk a horse with a rope in a corral. The horse was a magnificent thoroughbred, a golden sorrel with a white star on his forehead. The man with the rope came closer and gave Foal the rope. Foal was totally awed by the beauty and splendor in front of his eyes. He had never seen anything as magnificent in his whole life. It was majestic. It was a God-Horse.

Hesitantly he caressed the horse's coat and neck and head. All of a sudden, the horse stepped forward, put his head to Foal's chest, and nuzzled him in the most tender way. Foal heard himself whispering sounds of love.

Then the impossible happened. The God-Horse lifted his head, looked Foal straight in the eye, and went down on his knees in front of him, as in worship or prayer. Waves of infinite Love washed over him. Foal's heart felt like melting and expanding at the same time. Then the horse gently lay down on the soft turf, showing Foal his belly, never taking his eyes off Foal's. The belly was such a soft golden brown and white. It was a blessed moment.

～

Foal woke up in a stupor that gave way to this huge joy filling his heart, his every pore, his every breath. He never knew so much Love could exist, at least not inside him. Yet his mind was running wild with objections: how could such a thing be, how could a God-Horse lie down in front of him, kneel to insignificant, little him . . . preposterous! His mind simply could not conceive of it and stubbornly refused to accept it.

All of a sudden he was not alone anymore. There was this great hot Presence that Foal recognized as God Supreme. His head started resonating again.

So what happened, Foal? The Big One bowed to the little one? There is no little one, Foal. You are HUUUUGE. You just don't remember.

Is it so preposterous, Foal, that I, God, love you so much that I gave you life, that I knew I could trust the seed of life to grow in you? Preposterous is supposing it is not so. So life is precious Foal, and so are you.

He, the God-Horse, was bowing to the Great Being inside you that accepted in pure Love to be confined and limited in a minuscule body for the purpose of universal growth.

Your mind may be struggling now with this concept, but a few minutes ago, your heart seemed to have no problem accepting and melding with such pure emanation of Love.

The heart knows the greatness you hold, the greatness you are. The greatness of you bewilders your mind and recalls the Soul. It is the pure heart that urges the Soul to go back—the Love of Spirit that burns the Soul and inspires anguish to go back for reunion. So follow your heart and never doubt it. However big, however small you are, know your size is in the capacity of the heart.

So as you are
So do you choose
So shall you become.

Now, that was a lot to take in for poor little Foal, yet he could feel in his very bones the truth of it. God Supreme had volatilized again and he was left alone there to ponder the mysteries that felt so much bigger than him. But the glow of the dream was still with him, and the truth of what he had felt during it was so real that he could never doubt it.

Mmm, doubts. . . . Foal knew he had a problem with doubts. They were always present, always nagging at the back of his mind, spoiling even the best moments of bliss. And most unfortunately, his mind, as if of its own will, would always wander after them, running unconsciously on their trail. But he was feeling stronger by the moment, as if he was slowly gaining control of his doubts, of his very self. Like being more present . . . yes, "Present." Foal had heard this word before.

Foal knew there was actually a great buzz going around the world these days about being Present, being in the "Now." He had never really understood the concept fully, although he had tried hard to. He noticed how his disobedient mind was again wandering from one thought to the next, and then more random thoughts would distract it yet again.

Foal started wondering whether it would be too much to ask questions. He didn't want to overreach and then be judged as impatient or impertinent or . . .

The booming Voice stopped him in his tracks.

We never judge! And you are never to be judged.

It felt more like a sound than a voice, so big it was. It made the walls of his brain vibrate with potency. Who was this? No, not God Supreme, it didn't feel like Him. There was a more impetuous vibration to this sound. There was a feeling of great power, of discipline, and of affection.

Foal, this is Archangel Mika-el. I'll come back to you at another time. There is an angel here with me who literally is your answer. But first you have to formulate your question in clear, well-stated words, and it is to be said out loud.

Foal's mind was running wildly. Archangel Mika-el as in possibly Archangel Michael? Wow! Such a famous guy! But he knew inside that this was not the time for idle chatter; Foal decided to be direct and simply blurted out, "Please enlighten me, gracious angel; what does it mean to be in the **Now**?"

⌒ The Angel of Now ⌒

Foal, this is the Angel of Now. I am a feminine energy, because I talk of Home.

To be in the Now is to be Home.

Do you not see? When your thoughts wander, when you are distracted, when your worries take you to a future that still does not exist in your life, there is nobody Home.

When your guilt or regrets or nostalgias take you to a past that has ceased to exist in your life, there is nobody Home.

Your body feels like a shell—nobody Home.

Be Home.

Be in there, be in that moment, be in your body.

Inhabit your Soul-place, inhabit your Soul-body. Be there in each Now.

That is the meaning of Now.

To be Home is the moment of Now.

Be present in your body, fully inhabit your vessel. Inhabit your cells.

Be Home.

When I knock on your door, I expect you to be Home.

Welcome guests arrive when you're Home.

Waiting on them is your greatest pleasure.

They come from afar; they wish to find you Home.

You are "who-you-are" when you are Home.

Home is your center.

Home is the center of the universe, the center of you that is God.

Foal, will you be Home for me?"

Foal couldn't see her, but her suave, soft-spoken yet passionate voice painted a wondrous image in his mind. Foal decided right then and there that for such a beautiful feminine Being he would certainly be Home any time. He was grateful for her words of explanation and felt he was getting closer to grasping the concept itself. He knew she was telling him in very gentle words what a wandering mind his was.

"So Home is my center." thought Foal. "Each moment I must live in my center, must be conscious of the moment itself, no, of the moment **itself**."

That was enough for one day and for one night. He decided to let it sink in during sleep and ponder over it in the morning. He was hoping and praying that tomorrow would bring one more angel to him, but of course he could never be sure.

As the next night arrived, what felt like a huge angel came in a swirl of thought, like in a whirlwind. "Wow, this angel is definitely a guy," thought Foal. The angel felt so strong and powerful.

∼ Metatron ∼

This is Metatron, Foal. *Just to make things clear, let me add to the being in the Now subject. Linearity of thought can be unbalancing, because it obeys two polar opposites: a cause and an effect, a beginning and an end, a plus and a minus.*

But the moment of unlinearity is only **one**, *plus-minus zero; that is the Moment of* **Now**. *Forever in balance, forever existing, forever the minimum and the maximum of everything. Enjoy this blissful moment then; it is all you have and all you can ever do.*

The power is in the potential it holds.

The potential is in the power it is.

Live your moment of choice and do not take it for granted.

The moment of Now is the source of energy that changes the worlds.

As zero is the Now-moment of math, Now is the moment of creation.

The moment of choice, the moment of God's Choice.

Transmit these words.

Foal's mind was in a whirlpool. "Zero is the Now-moment of math?" His mind screamed, "What could it possibly mean? Why is he telling me this? And what did he say . . . 'to make things **clear**?' Was he joking?"

The angel seemed to hear him and spoke in a softer voice.

Foal, writing on paper things you don't understand is not easy. And now, since you've been asking, let us answer. Yes, as we told you. **Zero is the Now-moment of math.**

Think about the importance of being in the Now-moment of your energy, of your choice. That is where the energy and potential **is.** *That is the energy the zero holds for all your calculations. The energy of potential, the dimension of potential. Zero has the property of shifting from past to future, from future to past; but think this in mathematics. Zero in itself holds the great energy of adjustment. Zero is in the Now.*

Foal didn't dare to think because he knew he would be heard, yet he could not help wondering how "They" could think his little disconnected brain was ever going to make sense of all that. How much more gentle and easier had been the Angel of Now's words. More than ever he felt inadequate for this job! "God Supreme! Why is this coming to me? I am no big scientist or philosopher. Why did you choose me for your listener?"

God Supreme spoke out of nowhere.

Simply put, Foal, you were asking for it. And whether you know it or not, your Soul was pelting me with requests for permission. Furthermore, you have a big heart and that transcends any sort of rational knowledge. You shall be my Messenger.

"Great," mused Foal, "I must be very careful now about what I ask next time."

Foal! God Supreme boomed on, **It is not for anybody to see all the way through.** *But see the* **One** *illuminated place in front of you, and you'll go a long way. The Light will be shown one step at a time.*

A lantern shedding Light on the Way, step by step, cobblestone by cobblestone, illuminated one at a time. But that's all you need to have.

Keep the faith in you and don't look at the abyss.

*See only the **one illuminated stone**; your **Now** stepping stone.*

"For goodness sake!" Foal thought, a bit exasperated. "Even God was talking of **Now** now." He almost wished he had never asked. He decided to call it a night and get mentally ready for what the next day might bring.

~

The next angel was not an angel, or was he? He introduced himself as the Inner Child and had a twinkle and a trill in his voice.

⌁ The Inner Child ⌁

The child within you. Do not forget it.
The cry in you for joy, for help, for Love.
The offer of help, of joy, of Love.

The Friend, little but strong in its unique purity, the Angel of Light, the little Angel of Light.

I love to be loved and caressed, I love to be called sweet names, but this has nothing to do with ego. It's just the love of Love, the love of joy, the spring of life and laughter that never dries up in me. I am the ultimate purpose of your being. I am the One who first comes and first goes in your comings and goings.

What is the Light in you and where is the Light in you? It is my heart and it is in my heart. **A tiny flame can inspire another, a word of pity and consideration can mold a heart.**

See all the children around you. They need somebody to guide them. They need somebody-who-understands-them to guide them. They need somebody with love in the heart to lead them. Guidance is important, but how to guide is more important. Doing things and **how** to do them.

What is the feeling that engineers the thought and the action? **With what heart is the action done?** Is it a loving heart, is it caring, is it understanding, is it egoless?

So these are the questions of the children. They need to be assured, to feel protected, to feel embraced. So, lead the children, Foal, lead them on. They are the "new" generation, the new generation of such great import.

We are the propeller and the steering at the same time. We are at the back pushing and we are at the front leading.

I, your Inner Child, the Inner Child in you, the White one, the Joyful one, wish to have a say about this. The "I" in you would love to lead the children, to heal the children's hearts and show them the wonderful Way open to all who choose it.

Pick up your wings, feel your full self in the power of gentle me.

So it is in laughter I want to end, because laughter brings joy to the heart, relaxes the mind and the body, and enhances the Soul. **Seekers** we are and we shall be together.

And with a ripple of laughter reverberating in Foal's brain, the Inner Child was gone. Foal was left in the silence to ponder these thoughts. Foal liked this energy, the Inner Child, the "Love-Joy-Laughter-Help-the-Children" talk. Yes, this is something he could find in himself to do and that he could relate to.

A way to help the children, the Inner Child had said—the "new" children. Yes, that concept appealed to him, and what a difference it could make in the world! The new children, the new generation, the new children, the new children . . . .

And with such thoughts drifting in his mind, Foal fell asleep and was taken into the pure marvel of a dream.

◌ The Caterpillar-Kids Dream ◌

In the dream, an old friend, his wife, and their three kids had come to visit Foal. The young kids were so special. There was something different, but wonderful about them. Their features were not clearly defined, like they were blurred or just emerging from clay, but they were so cute Foal could find no words to describe them. He couldn't even tell whether they were boys or girls. Their mouths, noses, and eyes were just barely defined, only kind of vaguely distinguished from the rest of their faces, and their ears were more like two tiny protuberances.

The oldest was maybe 3 or 4 years old, the second was between 2 and 3, and the third, the most special and wonderful one, was possibly 7 or 8 months old. He was crawling on the floor, sliding out of a what looked like a sort of chrysalis. He looked more like a big caterpillar than a child. Yet he looked so adorable that Foal felt moved inside just by looking at him gently slithering out of his shell, and love welled up inside of him.

Foal was transfixed by the miracle unfolding in front of him and by the great sense of **Love** exuding from the children. There was something so terribly special and loving and sacred about them; like they were full of some Light emanating from within. They were aware.

He crouched in front of each one of them, feeling such great joy inside, that the words just burst out of him,

"I love kids!" Then, for some reason he didn't understand, he put his face close to their faces and sniffed, no, inhaled the air around each cheek, as if he had always greeted them this way, as if he wanted to breathe in or partake in their aura or essence. He felt this enormous bliss washing over him. Love flooded his heart. It was as if he had always known them. **Always.**

⌇

Then Foal abruptly woke up. Who were they? They had looked so familiar, but he couldn't place them. They certainly didn't look terrestrial. "Were they from another dimension of life . . . from another planet?" he considered. Yet to him, one thing was clear: he knew them and he knew them well. In the dream he had been so happy to see them again.

Again? Yes, again. Why "again"? How could he know the "new" generation, the generation to come? Wasn't it supposed to be "new"?

You surely know them, Foal. A resounding rush with a great force was filling his head.

Oh, thought Foal, I know this angel, I've met him before.

All throughout the universe is your Soul-family dispersed. You have lived many times, in many different forms, on many different planets, in different galaxies and dimensions. Some of the most enlightened Beings from such places are now gathering to Earth for its Clarion Call.

So the "new" generation is new, and extremely ancient at the same time. There will be many reunions Foal, get ready for them.

In your dream, they came to salute you, so that you may remember.

"I know you!" Foal blurted out. You are Archangel Mika-el!"

The big Energy laughed uproariously and said, *Good, so you are learning to tell Energy from Energy then, although it is actually all One and the same. Enchanted to see you, too, Foal. Still faithfully writing, I see.*

"So, what about those children then?" Foal boldly asked. "They were ETs?"

There are many ex-extraterrestrials on Earth now, Foal. You may be just one of them.

Foal was rendered speechless and stupidly repeated: "I, uh, am an ET? Like, uh, from another planet?"

⇝ Archangel Mika-el ⇜

S ouls learn in different dimensions at different speeds of growth. The whole universe is a big school for great learning and forever-going growth until you recall the God you are. There are many ET-Souls on planet Earth now. As humans, mind you, but they have been ETs in other existences before, on other planets they studied and grew. They have had different experiences from the human prior to this life.

And now those experiences are needed here on Earth for the Big Transformation to occur. You've seen the little one being born, being born . . . aware.

The caterpillar itself is a symbol for the Light-searching human, the transforming human. Those kids, they will be ready soon for the great flight, they are getting ready for the great metamorphosis . . . the human butterfly.

And with that, Archangel Mika-el was gone.

"Human butterfly. Mmm, interesting concept," mused Foal. "But what does it mean? Maybe one day I'll be growing wings, too, and I'll become an angel! I'd love that!" Foal smiled at this thought, realizing how little he had understood of all that Archangel Mika-el had said, except that there seemed to be ETs on Earth and that he may be one of them . . . fancy that! That struck him now as totally fantastic, and yet, were there such things as humans coming from other planets?

Well, another thing to sleep on and hope would be further clarified later. All in all, though, in spite of his not grasping all these new, quite outlandish concepts, Foal was actually enjoying the angels' talk immensely. He was thoroughly enchanted, despite his struggle to understand and to keep up with it all. Some of them spoke clearly enough, he pondered, but some could be truly mystifying and they left him with more questions than answers.

Yet, and yet again, all of them had one thing in common. They all spoke as if in a melody—magical wisdom words that felt like pure poetry to him, sweet lullabies that lured him into deep sleep more often than he cared for. He had, most regrettably, very often found himself totally unconscious on his precious notebook, and he felt so sorry for not having been able to stay awake through it all.

Foal made a mental note of this for the next time God Supreme decided to be around.

I AM always around, Foal! the big hot Voice boomed within the walls of his head. *Do you think I would ever leave you on your own? God forbid!* And then there was a big chuckle. *What would become of you? What would become of you all?*

Foal was once more taken aback by the suddenness of God Supreme's arrival. "Oh, hi . . . umm, hello, God Supreme. Good to see you, well, hear you again. I was just thinking . . ."

I know what you were thinking Foal. Indeed I do. So, say it out loud!

"Okay, then," mumbled Foal, "why is it that the angels address me in such poetic form that eventually puts me to sleep?" Foal could almost feel God Supreme's smile running through his own core.

Foal, the angels just love to sing! And as for you not being able to keep your head up, do not torture yourself over it. All is as it should be. Your brain needs to be in those resonating waves for you to be able to catch what they say. See how simple it all is? Rest at peace.

Foal felt greatly relieved at these words. He had been beating himself up over it for quite a while, and now he could see that there was a higher reason for this. He felt pleased with himself again and looked quickly around, wondering if, for once, he could catch a glimpse of God Supreme. Seeing, as usual, nothing, he let out a big sigh, whispering wistfully, "I so wish I could see You, my Lord, if only for just a millisecond, so I could make sure it is really You, and not me and my mushy brain talking to each other."

Foal, do not let your doubts overwhelm you again.

Know me for who I AM.

❧ God Supreme ❧

F oal, take note of this. **To love Me is to see Me everywhere.** In every ray, in every speck of dust, in every
smile, in every tear, in every face. If you love Me, you cannot
but **see** Me.

Now Foal, you have to write this and spread it to the
world, for there is hunger and there is thirst . . . the world is
famished for My Word. This kind of hunger is buried deep,
and it goes unnoticed until it explodes within and makes hearts
crave. Hearts pulsate again filled with longing, alive and conscious once more.

Feeling overwhelmed and a little sullen, Foal muttered
under his breath, "And You really think I can do this?"

You will try and you will see and you will know.

The Words of God have a long way to go.

And so God Supreme, chuckling to Himself, was
gone, once again, somewhere, and Foal didn't know how
to follow.

~

Foal had a dream that night, a very puzzling dream.

❧ The Baggage Dream ❧

He saw himself on a stage, and one of the staff there was telling him he had been chosen to receive a prize and he was to wait in line. Foal was very excited about this and had great expectations in his heart for the big moment to come. But by the end of the day, after waiting for a long time, everybody else was awarded, but he was not. It was such a blow to him. He had been expecting the prize so much, it was hard to let go of the thought.

He felt let down and betrayed, as if a huge hole had opened up in his heart, and in his great disappointment, he started purchasing things. Things, as in pretty heavy things, that he needed to drag around in big sacks from place to place with great difficulty. It seems he couldn't stop himself, and he was accumulating more and more by the day. Yet his disappointment would not go away; the big hole in his heart would not ever feel filled. He felt lonely and tired.

The scene then skipped and he saw himself going around and around in a small motorboat. He was travelling around a little rocky island in the middle of the ocean, but never seemed to get close to it. In his boat were loads and loads of fruits and vegetables. All the produce was very heavy. He was looking at the produce and feeling what a heavy burden it had all been to him along his journey. He was finally seriously thinking of throwing it all away. But he had a companion with him now, and it seemed that this person was not yet willing to let go of the load.

This time, however, Foal would not be dissuaded. There was this frenzy building up inside him that he couldn't keep down. He said, "Listen, we have to get rid of all this, it is squashing us." And then, without waiting for an answer, he stood up in the rocking boat and started to throw everything overboard.

There he was! From a vantage point up in the air, he could see himself throwing everything out with a vengeance: a big cabbage, then apples, melons, pumpkins, huge turnips—you name it. Then, turning his face up to the blue sky, he yelled at the top of his lungs:

"I learned my lesson well!

I learned my lesson well!

I LEARNED MY LESSON WELL!"

And with these words in his mouth, he woke up. He was mystified. To whom was he yelling? And with such vehemence! And why was he yelling? Why not just say the words? Besides, it was almost hilarious to watch his tiny self screaming at the empty sky! But deep in his heart Foal felt upset by this dream. The heavy luggage he was carrying around did ring a bell.

In the dream it felt as if whenever he had a disappointment in life, he would try to fill this hole in his heart by acquiring things, and he would pile up any kind of unresolved issues, consequently accumulating all sorts of unhealthy thoughts; all this was making his journey forward so difficult and tiring that he was on the verge of giving up. Yes, he could understand how true the dream was, and how enlightening it was for him to be able to observe himself actually acting out his life. What a clever way to show him and make him see what was going on in his life. This must be Angels' School, he thought. Cool! Absolutely cool!

Yet the last part again. . . .What was he doing? Why was he screaming so loudly? He looked around hoping somebody would be there to answer this, but he was greeted with only silence. "Maybe next time," he thought, "I'll have a chance to ask about this too."

The next night, though, such a big angel arrived that he totally forgot about it. Actually, he wasn't an angel exactly. He announced Himself as the Christ.

⌒ The Christ ⌒

The Love of Spirit inside is to be cherished, fanned and ventilated, to be lit in a flame of passion.

Passion for all human beings, for all life on this Earth.

Compassion for all human beings, for all life on this Earth.

Life in the human, life in the animal, life in the plant, in the rock, in the water, in the air.

Turn ego into compassion, Foal.

Life is sacred as Spirit is.

Respect the sacredness, respect the Spirit in it, in every tiny part of it.

Remember My dying on the cross for you.

Remember My spilling the blood of the Christ to raise Earth's and people's consciousnesses.

As a blessing, as a lifting, as a teaching, to show the Way, the way back to the Father Mother God of Creation.

The seeds were sown in My blood, now they will bloom in your Love, the Love that all humanity is nurturing in order to take the great step.

Spread the message, Foal, the message of Love.

The poor in Spirit are not to be left behind. As we are taking care of you, take care of them.

Unwillingly you must not go on this path.

From the depth of your being you would feel the need and ecstasy to go on.

Ecstasy of Spirit burning in all its glory and beauty.

The great purity of the Soul merging with its Source.

I AM Love.

This I came to tell you all and it still is My message to you.

Love brings abundance of heart, for Love is the most abundant energy of all.

Abundance of heart is needed to get abundance in your life.

Abundance as ripeness of feelings, abundance as filling and compassionate, abundance as joy and laughter, abundance as Love overflowing.

Forgiveness is part of your abundance,
In forgiveness you'll find joy,
In forgiveness you'll find Love overwhelming,
In forgiveness you'll find yourself.

It is only Love that it is needed,
It is only Love that it is lacking,
It is only Love that can fill the heart of a lonely one, the heart of one who is looking for Spirit, but can't find his way about it.

Love is all-pervading, Foal, and it starts from your heart.

When everything else is gone, I stay.
I AM the Source and I AM the Way.

≈

"Oh, how do you respond to this?" Foal thought. He was left in a blissful stupor. It felt as if a wave of Love and warmth had been poured over him. He had never given thought to Love in such way. In such a total enthusiastic way. And forgiveness. That was something he had tried hard to integrate into his life, but to forgive hurtful things that had been done to him, well, that had not come easily, although he dared hope that he had been successful to a certain degree. He had done his best after all; he had tried hard—or had he?

Once again he felt the hot Presence of God Supreme suddenly there.

Love, abundance, forgiveness. Forgiveness. . . . What do you know of forgiveness, Foal? Have you forgiven the slights done to you, have you forgiven yourself for the slights you brought upon others? Forgiveness—it is truly the truth and valor of a Soul.

Foal felt a bit uncomfortable hearing these words. He was not sure he had been able to truly forgive. And it wasn't the big offenses that bothered him; actually, it felt more as if it were the little slights that still needed to be resolved.

"Lord, I am not sure I have been able to forgive myself for all, but I have tried, although maybe not perfectly, to forgive others—at least those that I remember."

Those that you remember?

Foal, you will have truly forgiven only when you have truly forgotten.

"Forgotten? But, excuse me, God Supreme, with all due respect, how can I forget? I can forgive, maybe, but I can't forget. How could I possibly forget?"

You can recall the deed, Foal, but not recall the emotions.

"Ooh, I see. . . ."

Foal had a true moment of clarity. For the first time, he could easily see how it would be all right to remember what actually happened, if all the negative emotions involved, such as spite, jealousy, guilt, and retaliation, were not recalled with it.

You see, Foal? You do? That is truly an enlightened statement. Indeed, it is not easy to see this truth.

"I mean," added Foal, "I understand what You are saying, but I still don't see how we manage to not recall the emotions."

Well, for a start, by letting go, by releasing the anger, the grief, the disappointment, the guilt, the remorse, the frustration; by forgetting the perpetrator and the victim at the same time; by freeing yourself of chains that fetter the heart, such as emotional memories, by . . .

"Oh!" Foal unexpectedly burst out laughing. "By throwing all the baggage out of the boat!"

*Yes, Foal! **Yes!** By throwing all the baggage out of the boat, all that is keeping you down—**out of the boat!** Exactly! And last but not least, be grateful for the knowledge received through the very deed that hurt you the most.*

"Okay, okay, I am getting it. I can see the meaning of the dream in a more lucid way now. But now that we talk of the dream, may I ask why I was shouting so loudly to the sky?"

Mmm, Foal, as for that, go back into your dream, ask your dream for clarification, try to recall something very important that it seems you missed when you were waking up.

And His voice vanished again into thin air.

Foal, mumbling to himself, repeated God Supreme's words: "'Go back into your dream. . . .' Easy to say, but how does one go back into a dream?" Well, all these profound insights and truths that were being "poured" into him proved at times difficult to absorb. He felt happy, privileged, and honored, and yet at the same time, he was exasperated at his own inadequacy.

Foal felt he needed some more time to put his mind in order, so he decided once again to wait for tomorrow's angel to possibly and hopefully clarify.

The next angel he encountered was one he already knew and for whom he felt profound love. This angel arrived, as always, in all his impetuous glory.

☙ Archangel Mika-el ☙

Thank you, Foal, for listening to the little voice inside. Thank you, for taking notice and notes.

In the heart of a little human lies the seed of a huge star. In the magic moment of Oneness you'll realize and perceive the perfection of something so seemingly imperfect. The mission of the human is to uncover the seed, wake the seed, let it grow in all of its glory. The seed in you is one of our family. You are one of mine, Foal.

Foal's eyes snapped open. "I am?"

"Yes, I AM." replied the Archangel.

Foal was a bit put off by this answer, so very tentatively, he sputtered, "I am? You mean, you are."

Yes, Foal. I AM. insisted Archangel Mika-el.

"Okay, if you say so."

*I AM, Foal, **I AM.***

Puzzled to the extreme, but respectfully obliging, Foal whispered, "I AM." Then the great angel went on saying something so unexpected and unimaginable that it took Foal totally by surprise and almost threw him into a fit.

Good then, said the archangel, *from now on, you shall call me Lord Michael, as I AM your liege.*

For a fragment of a second Foal's mind went silent. How could such a thing be said so nonchalantly, and as if in passing? Oh my, oh my! Foal could not contain himself, his mind felt like bursting. Wow, wow, **wow**! Foal's heart was exploding with joy and excitement and what else? Oh so much "else"! "I can call you Lord Michael? Really? And you are my liege? Like I belong to you? Oh, my! Wow, wow! Oh my, oh **my**!"

OK now, you are so totally losing your brain waves. Quiet down and listen carefully.

⌒ Lord Michael ⌒

F*oal. . . . (big pause) Now, listen well. Listen closely. The authenticity of the core Being . . .*

When one leaf at a time is peeled off of you, there stands an angel, naked in its beauty, full of light and splendor, made of Love.

Go see your Soul naked, take away the layers with which you have clothed it. See the purity in itself, crystal-pure, unadorned because more beauty could not be added. There is no fear there, no need for comparisons, for expectations, no place for ego. Only Self in its purest pristine form exists. The I AM species.

It has not been put there to hide, rather to be discovered and carved out of all the junk accumulated in lifetimes of wanderings. And one "discovered" Soul can discover many others, so more and more can find God, the Supreme Source, the only Source, the Creator of All, and of all "Selves."

**There is only one God
with no name and only Presence,
and that is the God of all.**

There is beauty in other people's souls that you can grow, as there is beauty in your Soul that you can make grow.

In the process lies the secret. The process of growing, of evolution.

There are many bells in the heart of the human; they ring from time to time to awaken a soul, to warn a soul, to push up a soul, to let him/her hear the sound of the Call. Follow the Call of your Soul. Follow the trumpet of God, the God inside you, the God outside you, the One **who is All** and **that is All**.

So let the bells ring in your heart; let them awaken your Soul. Let them remind you of the promises you made, of the missions you chose. Foal, can you not rejoice in your Soul? How can you not rejoice in your Soul?

In a world of mesmerizing beauty lives the Soul, unencumbered by layers of duties and fetters, just too pure to compromise with human reality.

All the things I say, you already hold in your heart. Star seed that you are.

Find the Love of God in you,

Find the Love of God.

And just as soon as he had arrived, he left in the blink of an eye.

∾

"Hmm . . . ," mused Foal. "'How can you not rejoice in your Soul,' Lord Michael says. But I do, I do rejoice in my Soul. Yet, where is it? Where is my Soul? Where and how can I find it, such a beautiful Soul?"

Foal wanted to give more thought to this concept, but his mind was entirely preoccupied with something else. There was something nagging him and he didn't know how to let it go. It was God Supreme's words that he had been missing something, that he had to go back into the dream . . . right! The baggage dream was really bugging him. He had still not gotten an answer either from dreams or angels. So, what had he been missing? What was God Supreme trying to point out? And how do you go back into a dream?

"Whatever!" he thought. "Let me try the only thing that I have in my power to do."

~

So, with that resolve in his mind, that night, he made a point to express his desire for clarification and to see what happened . . . well, to see if anything at all happened! So before he went to sleep, he prayed. "Please, take me where I can be taught and remember, and I can come back and remember."

And that night, indeed, Foal got his clarification dream. Such a bizarre dream.

Little Dot Dream

He was suspended in space, watching this peculiar scene unfold in front of his eyes in such a strange landscape, the likes of which he had never seen before. There were two planes where the action was taking place. One was the "above" plane, which was like a station platform for arrivals and departures; and the other, the "below" plane, was possibly the Earth plane. There were many tiny black dots coming and going from one plane to the other in a very busy way—coming and going, coming and going.

He knew he was one of the dots and that all of them, after duly receiving instructions, were kind of diving into this "below" place. Foal could not see who was giving the instructions, but he knew they were the Big Teachers. When his turn came, they explained to him how once "down there," his job was to remember, to learn to remember, just that.

They went on warning that they would send experience after experience to help him remember, and if he didn't, they would keep sending the same experience all over again, until he did. The little dot that was Foal felt certain he had understood everything and he was quite confident that he could do this. Consequently he dived in, incarnating in a life again.

Once there, the little dot did get his share of "experience"; it was pretty heavy stuff indeed, but he felt sure that he had managed to learn and remember. He was actually proud that he had been able to do his job as told.

Quite happy with himself, he went back "Up there," and, after a short while, he was sent into another life again. This time, the little dot that was Foal felt pretty cozy and smug inside, knowing that he had overcome the learning "experience." He was looking forward to having an easier life this time around.

But lo and behold! He got exactly the same experience he thought he had already mastered. He was so disappointed and surprised at the same time, and he could not understand why everything was the same. He had definitely remembered to remember, he felt he had learned his lesson, he had gone through all the hardships and seen through them. Then, **why**? Why did he have to go through it all again? It was totally unfair.

So when it was his time to go back "Up there," he rushed to his Teachers and protested: "I did all you told me to do. Why did you send me the same experience all over again?"

And so the Teachers told him, *But you have to say it. You have to say it out loud.*

So the poor little dot dived in there again and he had to go through the same experience once more, but this time he was furiously thinking and repeating to himself as if in a craze: "I have to say it out loud, I have to say it out loud, I must remember to say it out loud, otherwise it will happen again, I don't want it to happen again, I don't want it to happen again!" and then he shouted, "I learned my lesson well!"

The watching Foal could not help but laugh. "It is so totally hilarious watching myself from above," he thought. He considered how the little dot was him, all right, but also how from this vantage point he felt some sort of distance, some space that gave him clarity. And yet the little dot that was Foal, well, wasn't he serious about it!

As his dot's time came and he had to go back "Up there" again, he ran to the Teachers and blurted out in one big breath, "I learned, I learned my lesson well! I learned how it is the power of experience and pain that helps us remember, no, no, rather the power of emotions most of all. **Yes**, this is what we have to learn—the power that strong emotions generate brings us to final understanding and remembering."

$\sim$

And still quite breathless, Foal woke up. Wow, this Angels' School was getting tough. His head was in a whirlpool once again, as he tried to make order of all the various insights that were flashing simultaneously through his mind. His head felt tightly packed with new understandings and totally nebulous at the same time.

Then, for an instant, the smoggy clouds in his head parted and he saw it. Since the very beginning, the angels and God Supreme Himself had been constantly asking him to state his questions out loud, just as the Teachers in the dream had instructed him to do. "Got it" he thought. "For whatever reason, it seems it is of the utmost importance to do so." Very good to know! It would spare him quite a few trials, but he still couldn't grasp the reason why. "I must remember to ask about this the next time I have a chance to," mused Foal.

Yet now he could finally understand why, in the Baggage Dream, he had been so furiously shouting at the sky in the first place. He surely had a reason for that! A good reason! All that load of, so to speak, "experience" so very graciously sent to him so he could learn to remember, was something he certainly didn't want to go through again! Hmm . . . but **hey!** Wait a moment. Something really didn't add up. How could he have known about it in the Baggage Dream? He had not yet had the Little Dot Dream at that time. He had no way of knowing about this.

The order of the dreams was definitely not right, he concluded. Okay, one more thing to add to the pile of his multiplying questions. With this thought in his mind, he drowsily slipped into sleep again.

∾

The next morning, Foal was startled awake by God Supreme's sudden words.

Some pretty strong statements you were making in there, Foal. Would you care to expand for me? What was the lesson you learned after all?

Foal quickly scrutinized the air around him to see if he could get a glimpse of God Supreme, but Divinity was as elusive as ever. Albeit still drowsy from sleep, he was prompt in answering, because the dream was still vivid and alive under his skin. So he was confident when he replied:

"I learned that it is the power of emotions that brings us closer to the God in us and eventually to **You**, Lord. I understood that it is the big traumas, more often than not, that give us space to think, . . . to feel, no, not exactly feel, . . . to go inside and remember, remember who we truly are, see through the scheme, find the One we are."

Hmm, what a messy explanation, Foal.

"Wait, wait!" Foal blurted out in one breath "I'll try again, I know what I felt. I **know** what I felt. It is just not easy to put it into words."

"OK," continued Foal, "It is as if we are going through these many lives, repeating experience after experience, until we see through them. We can accomplish this only through our heart-felt emotions. Through them, and their intensity, we come to understand and to remember who we really are, and so we can break the cycle . . . I suppose."

Foal was running out of breath and words, but this other "big" thought kept coming up till it burst out:

"Oh, yes! **Emotion is the great engine of the universe!**

"Emotion = Energy

"I can feel this Teaching in my bones, heart, what-ever! I understand the power of emotion and I under-stand how 'impact' experience brings it about."

That is better Foal, commented God Supreme, *and I can see how you heed the message of the dreams.*

"Yes, I do, God Supreme, I really do! When I am in there, it is so easy to understand, because I experience all, I live it from the inside out and the lessons go straight to my heart. But it seems, though, that when we learn a les-son, it is not enough to understand it. We have to say it out loud, right? **Why?** Why out loud?"

God Supreme took a few moments before answering, as if to give Foal time to gather his energy and quiet down.

⊱ God Supreme ⊰

F oal, the unraveling of sound makes the cosmos appear and
disappear.

Sound has the power of creation.

Sound **is** the power of creation.

The power of pure manifestation is in the sound.

The whole creation is a reverberation of energy.

All life is a dance of vibrations, a symphony of sounds.

Sound can bypass "boundaries" of dimensions.

Sound carries a longer way than you would know, Foal.

Sound gives you the power to manifest, to create.

"My" manifestation, "your" manifestation, it is all one
and the same.

Your own sound, your own frequency, is your own signa-
ture in manifesting.

So to manifest your power of creation, use your sound,
Foal. Yes, say it out loud.

A vague understanding started to take shape in Foal's
mind, but he couldn't articulate it. It felt like he almost
understood but couldn't quite grasp it. So he said in a
whisper: "I will, God Supreme, I will." A few moments
passed and Foal started fidgeting; he still had one more
question, but God Supreme's silence made him uneasy.
Yet he knew he would not be at peace until he asked. So,
a little hesitantly, he went on. "Hmmm, about the dream,
God Supreme . . . would you care to, uh, talk some more?

I am always game, Foal. What is it? And, were you happy with your clarification dream?

"Hmm, yes . . . and no."

Oh? How so?

"Well," he said and then stopped. How do you make a point to Divinity? he thought. Foal inhaled deeply before exhaling in one big breath. "God Supreme, I have found an incongruity."

An incongruity? Hmm . . . interesting; let's hear it.

And so Foal went for it. "God Supreme, the dreams' order is upside down!" There! he had said it. Big gulp. Foal felt funny in the center of his chest. God Supreme's Light felt like it was beaming many little rays into his heart. Was this . . . ? God . . . laughing? The big Voice felt totally amused.

Imagine that! You're such good sport, Foal! Of all the many good lessons in that dream, you had to go and pick up on the order of the dreams.

Foal felt abashed and sputtered defensively, "Not only that, of course! But the time doesn't add, you see. The time of the dreams should be reversed!"

*The Time, the **time**! What time? Time exists only in your mind, Foal. Dreams do not necessarily follow "your" time-line. Bear with them, will you? Understand with the heart, accept the message you feel inside without too many analytical questions.*

Time is everywhere. Everywhere. It could never be contained in a line. The line that Time is to your mind does not exist. As there are dimensions of space, there are dimensions of time.

Time and timelessness all at once.

It's all happening and it has not happened yet.

What was and what will be IS.

Didn't you understand Metatron's message to you at all? Try to go back and see what he was trying to tell you.

Foal's throat felt suddenly tight as he struggled with his thoughts.

Well, well! continued God Supreme, *do you not look rather confused.*

Time then for some more angels' talk and their inspiring clarifications, right? So, shall we ask the angels to come to you again? At their own timing of course! Angels' time, Foal! Angels' time! Could be "upside down," you know . . .

And with his usual chuckle His Presence vanished in the air again.

Foal was mortified and embarrassed at his own stupidity. Something tugged at his memory. He remembered too late Metatron's message on linearity, actually unlinearity. How there is only the **Now**. So no past or future there? His eyebrows pulled together in mystification. How was he supposed to understand this? Yes, he definitely needed some more clarification.

∾

As night approached, Foal started to feel a bit apprehensive. He wondered whether he would indeed be able to keep up with the profundity of the words of the angels. He felt so small, there was so little of him, so very little. It was pointless to teach him, he was no scientist, no philosopher, no great mind, no anything. How was he supposed to understand; how could he keep up with all they were striving to pass through to him? Such wasted effort. . . . He was afraid to blunder again, and to feel stupid again, and especially, he was afraid to disappoint them. Concepts such as "time is everywhere," "sound is the power of creation," and "zero is the Now," were so alien to him that his brain was going numb just trying to contemplate them. He was in dire need of reassurance as he felt his inner energy vacillating. He felt alone, dejected, forlorn. Nonetheless, although he didn't know it yet, just what his spirits needed was already on his way.

In fact, that night a joyful, vibrant angel arrived in a buoyant swirl and most enthusiastically smiled into his head. He whispered that he was his companion angel and that he had been with him since the beginning of time.

He introduced himself as Emmanuel. *Call me EM*, he said. And Foal, in feeling the very first sound of the harmonious Love-voice resonating in his head, felt instantly and so inexplicably serene and totally at peace.

☙ Angel EM ❧

I AM the Powerful One, but also the bringer of peace. I AM your companion angel. I have been with you always. Companions of lives indeed. Me to you and you to me.

So now, what is it with you? Do I see confusion? Things are not as clear as they should be? Oh, but they are! They are evolving. It is the evolution in their station that you can't see.

Awakenings are for wise people in disguise. What disguise did you come up with to hide the wise man inside? The timing of awakening is most wondrous indeed. Wisdom hidden in the soul comes forth at the most appropriate time and the knowledge of it is revealed to that very being in many different states.

To be incarnated is an incredible process. Arduous, incredibly so, but rewarding, incredibly so.

The joys of a human can reach Spirit and touch heaven. The depth of Love in a human is the Spirit it holds inside.

When you came into this plane, you didn't remember. Now you are recalling, and you don't always like it, and you always doubt it. The enchantment of a life to live again is alluring for all souls who have known the Earth plane. In spite of the bewildering challenges you well know you may have to go through, you all feel this irresistible urge to go back. You want so badly to finish and fulfill what you set out to do. The desire of proving to oneself, "Next time I'll do better," always beckons.

But the great forgetting is all powerful indeed. Raise the great angel in you that is you, the Being who chose to come here to accomplish miracles.

All is there to understand, not judge.

To understand is to know to be One, to know you are One.

Trust and allow the flow of Love inside you and through you, allow the energy of the universe to bring information into you.

So be open and be free and ask your questions.

There is no question that cannot be truly answered.

The gateway to universal information is inside you.

Ask your questions in the spirit of Love, compassion, and gratitude.

Love is the basis-energy of **All**.

Compassion encompasses **All** and makes you one with **All**.

Gratitude is the great gift of Love that you receive from the universe and have to give back to the universe multifold.

You cannot trust inspiration if you do not trust yourself.

It is all in the perception of the perspective.

A different perception uncovers a different you.

This will take you to the place where you can trust what is being given through you, and it will take you there where you can trust what you are writing down.

Let me be your companion of Light, your staff on the way, the one to be with you in your joy and in your sorrow.

Let me be your Light that shines in the dark of all the darkest hours, in the dark of the darkest path.

The Love you feel for me and the Love I feel for you is one and the same.

Know me as you've always known me.

Know me for what I've always been.
Know me for your true and faithful companion along the
journey.

I am Emmanuel.
God with me.

~

Foal felt happy. After his great embarrassment with God
Supreme, he reveled in the uplifting, reassuring energy of
this angel, his companion angel. How sweet, how deli-
cious could that be . . . He felt spellbound, hanging on
every word EM had said to him. His eyes were moist. He
dabbed at his tears, thinking how deeply the angel's words
had touched him. "I am not alone," he drowsily thought,
"no one is alone." And thus with a calm, soothed heart,
he drifted into one more dream—a very short, but mean-
ingful dream.

⌒ The Body-Suit Dream ⌒

Foal could see himself looking into a room full of rows
of chairs, and on one chair, there was some sort of
deflated balloon in the form of a human body sitting
inanimate, but leaning forward, draped over the chair
in front of it. It was a bright, orange-pink color, and it
seemed to be made of some quite thick rough rubber, like
a diving wet suit but complete with a head and feet. A
rubber body suit, a strange, deflated human balloon. He
instinctively knew it was something he had to put on, but
then his attention got distracted by some voice in the air
saying words that sounded important, but which, unfortunately, he forgot.

∽

He woke up sensing that he had lost various segments
and meanings of the dream. However, he was sure the
rubberish deflated balloon represented the empty shell of
a human body, the mask he thought we were all supposed
to "put on" each time we incarnate into a different life.

As he was musing over these thoughts, the big Presence of God Supreme emerged once again. Still groggy
from his deep sleep, Foal managed a feeble "Hello" and
then quietly, hoping for approval, he said, "That is our
body, right?" God Supreme thundered back:

"That-is-what-you-think-you-are, Foal!"

Amazing, right? How could anyone in his right mind assume such a thing? Yet you do. It is what duality does to you and still, it is just because of this that the human experience is valid.

Will you be able to see through the veil of duality from inside the dark, thick depth of that body suit? Will all your trials elevate you to the point you'll be able to see into it? This is a tantalizing feat indeed. Circumstances can be very challenging, but you can hold them at bay, watching them relentlessly, without judgment, without interpretation. Just watch and watch, and realize you are watching.

Realize you are watching and you are the player.

By becoming the observer, you will find that place, hmm . . . how did you call it, Foal? That "vantage point" up there from where you watch yourself in a dream. It was actually brilliantly put, I must say.

Yes, the "observer" point, the distance that gives you clarity of vision so you need not identify with the situation. So you need not suffer again.

Foal became suddenly alert. "Brilliantly?" That seemed to be the only word he caught of the whole long speech. God Supreme answered with a smile.

Yes, Foal, brilliantly.

"Ooh!" Foal was at an utter loss for words. He felt happy and a tiny bit smug inside. "Thank God!" he mused, "At least I got that one right . . . OOPS!" He suddenly remembered how his thoughts were always broadcast through a megaphone these days, and hurriedly tried to mentally back pedal. Too late.

God Supreme had, of course, caught on to his little mindlessness in no time and was already playfully replying: *Your thanks are always welcome, Foal. Nevertheless, I* would deeply appreciate it if you paid more attention to the rest of all I am saying to you.

"Right. Sure. . . ." stammered Foal. "You were talking about the vantage point, the observer point."

Mmm, so you were getting something after all, commented God Supreme, *apart, of course, from your own brilliancy. Yes, you must learn to disconnect.*

"Disconnect?" repeated Foal. "How can I disconnect?"

You can pick up and acknowledge only the emotion and not the fact.

"What?" spluttered Foal, totally flabbergasted. In one big lunge, he was sitting upright on the bed. "But you said before that we can recall the deed, but not the emotions!"

And so it is. Never the two together. By isolating either one, you become the observer. The space, the distance . . . the clarity! Disconnect one from the other and get yourself a perspective, Foal. Pick either one and observe.

Now, back to your "Body-Suit Dream" . . . and this is important, important and controversial, so hear me out attentively. It is all about growth, see, and it is love that makes you grow. Or, as you justly put it—again, another brilliant insight, I will say—if it is grief and pain that you need for your evolution, that is what you will get. Because that is what **you** *would want. As simple as that.*

The process of incarnation is all about evolution, which is to say, waking the big Spirit inside, polishing it until it can be seen shining even from the outside of that all-obscuring body suit. It takes more than one human to make a Soul.

God Supreme vanished again and Foal was left looking around rather dumbly. It was all so very much beyond him, he thought. The depth, the profundity he sensed, far surpassed all he could ever hope to comprehend; nevertheless, God Supreme's words penetrated to his core. He was well aware that he was still struggling to understand all he was being taught, but he also knew how determined he was to keep up. There was this burning desire to not let down his Lord. "Hmmm," he thought. "I must start by getting myself a perspective, then. How do I do that?"

In a dream it was pretty easy to watch himself from a distance and keep the perspective, but in real life, that seemed almost impossible. His feelings always so overwhelmingly possessed him. Yes, totally, totally possessed him. How could he free himself? Would he ever be able to get free from his own self?

And just as that thought was formed, a voice, filling with air the lungs of his mind, whispered in a soft blow as only the wind could:

When you reach your freedom, you reach Spirit in you.

Foal almost jumped out of his skin. What was that? Who was that? This was different! While the angels' messages always started and resonated deep inside his head, the voice that was filling his mind now seemed to originate from a space near the ceiling of his room. This voice originated outside himself and inside himself at the same time! How could this be? It felt as if his mind was inhabited by someone—someone who was not him. And that was scary.

He shook his head, trying to dislodge that weird feeling. He turned around and around, stealing quick glances here and there, vainly searching the empty air. There were times when he thought things were getting kind of out of hand. He worried he was receiving more than he had bargained for . . . much more! Would he be able to cope with all that?

Nevertheless, he instinctively knew that once you open that door, there is no turning back. "Besides, who would want to turn back?" he thought. He would not ever, **ever** want to turn back. Anyway, he considered, that had not been an option from the beginning. He told himself not to be stupid and get scared at this point of the journey; rather, he should be prepared for all that may be sent his way.

He took a few seconds to sort all this out and then decided he would take some rest, pull himself together, and wait for the next angel to come and bring his wisdom through to him. And even if he couldn't understand, he contemplated, he knew he could trust. And trust seemed to him as good a starting point as any.

And as it was, that night a beautiful, suave, wise angel came—the Archangel Chamuel.

∾ Archangel Chamuel ∽

This is Chamuel, Foal. The Archangel. The Third Sacred Ray.

It is the complete trust inside that makes the momentum and the impact.

Ooh! These words were said in such a strong, clear, elegant way that Foal found himself totally enthralled with their intense beauty. The Archangel continued:

Trust and allow.

Allow Spirit to work through you.

Allow yourself to be yourself,

Allow yourself to do the deeds you still don't dare.

My message to you tonight is one of empowerment.

Take the power in your hands and consume it.

For once, throw yourself into the doing of the deed to be done.

Dare your Soul to the utmost moment of bliss.

Dare your Soul to know who you are.

Dare your mind and body to the extremes of the paradox of life, without hurting them in the least.

Audacity is to dare, but not overdo.

Sacredness in the heart is kept, in the heart it is first felt.

But it will take you all: your body, your mind, your Soul.

Sacred is profound.

Profound is sacred.
So the teachings are.
So the great awakenings are.
We rejoice in that.
We celebrate the time of Resurrection.
The time of he/she who is Light.

Give Light to all the Beings who do not feel they hold
it inside.
Give Light to the poor in Spirit, because they don't know
they have it.
Give Light to the world to rejoice in the Cosmic Circle
of Life.

In one way or the other, you'll get there where you have
made yourself a promise to go.
You'll experience what is your wish to fulfill and you will
die of joy in it.
The phoenix in you is not afraid to be burnt by that fire.
The dragon slayer in you will conquer the fear of the
dragon.
When fear is conquered, the dragon can be ridden . . .
It is only in the Light of God that we are strong.
Only in the name of Spirit can we conquerrrrrrrrrrrrrrr . . .
ooooooohhhhhhh . . .

And with such a strange echo left behind, he was gone.

Foal was stunned; he was so choked up with gratitude
that he could hardly speak. He felt such a great Love of
Spirit burning in his heart, surging up in him, welling
up from inside, and for some unfathomable reason, the
words flowed out of him so unexpectedly, so naturally.

"I understand," he said, "Spirit knows how to remember Spirit even when in a human body. I need to show

you that. I will show you that. I will remember the Spirit in me more and more. Spirit can do all, Spirit can be all. There is no challenge it cannot take! I will take the power in my hands and consume it. I can't possibly claim to understand all, but I do understand this, that I can do this, that I am supposed to do this, that I came to do this."

And with these words still hot in his mind, he drifted off into sleep. The dream he found himself in was so very different from all the others and so totally unanticipated.

∽ The Demon Dream ∾

Foal saw himself traveling abroad to attend a spiritual event. As he stepped into his hotel room, a middle-aged lady, quite nice, petite, with short blond hair, came into the room and started explaining about the hotel. Probably hotel staff, he assumed. They started chatting and Foal explained about the sacred event he was going to attend and, unexpectedly, he found himself encouraging her to participate as well.

Foal strongly felt in his heart that he would really like for her to have a chance to open her heart to the Light, to find the Divinity inside. He talked about all the incredible things that could happen at such gatherings and added, "Things are different for every person; still, it will be good to be there."

As he said this, he saw this lady, who was now sitting on a couch in front of him, lower her head, and cover her face with a newspaper. Foal assumed she must have somehow gotten emotional. But as he looked on, he noticed that her right hand, which was resting on the arm of the sofa, was withering and drying up; it was slowly turning brown and the fingers were becoming long and bony with long dirty nails.

When he looked up at her face again, she had lowered her newspaper and was sneering at him. Her face had withered too and her eyes were two black holes in a contorted, shriveled face. And staring him straight in the eyes, with a sneer, she said: **"I got you now!"**

And Foal, who should have been scared or terrified to death to say the least, could not find fear in himself. He sat there, very still, looking at her, feeling this overwhelming sense of peace coming over him. Staring into those sunken, hollow, terrible eyes, he quietly said:

"Good. I am ready for you. God is with me. Spirit is with me. I am ready."

He woke up elated with these words still repeating in his mind: "I am ready. God is with me. I am ready." He felt so happy inside and still in such bliss that he had no words to describe the way he felt. Yet, he was absolutely baffled by the power of the dream and totally astonished by his own reaction. Did he really say that?

He couldn't believe it. Normally he would have been cowering in front of such a ghastly apparition. It should have been a horror dream, nightmarish, like seeing the devil that had come for you. What could be worse or more terrifying? Yet he mysteriously and absolutely knew the demon had no power over him.

For some reason he felt blissfully stronger than he had ever felt in his whole life and ready for any challenge. He felt empowered by this dream and intuitively knew he owed this new-found strength to the angels. At the same time, Foal was getting confused by all kinds of different emotions welling up in him.

So what, what was truly disturbing him? Well, the demon, yes, for sure, that was the one thing disturbing him the most; it was disturbing in different ways, and for inexplicable reasons. He went further inside himself to get in touch with his feelings more, to see if he could find anything close to fear, anger, or hatred toward this demon, but, surprisingly, he could not. On the contrary, he found pity for that lady, whom he had actually thought could be "saved" or shown the Way to the Light.

He was amazed and surprised when he became aware it was compassion, rather, that filled his heart. What a mind-blowing, overwhelming thing to realize! The big voice of God Supreme shook him out of his reverie.

Well done, Foal, well done! To find compassion in such extreme circumstances is the ultimate proof of Spirit being freed inside you. Your Soul spoke for you at such deep depth that it will not be ignored, cannot be ignored. That's who you truly are, invincible, fearless, egoless. So I commend you and I praise you for your great commitment, for the declaration of the truth of who you are, for your readiness to meet the Shadow.

By the way, do not get carried away. It is no devil or demon, as you seem to have hastily concluded; it is no satanic being you may dread or fancy about. Shadow is a part of you, part of your own innumerable fragmentations, negative energy formed in many lives. Shadow belongs to you, Foal, and needs to be integrated into you to make you whole again.

*Whole as **All IS**. Thus your Soul was inviting it to the Light. Thus you felt compassion. Shadow is there to hinder you, to hamper your growth. Yet in doing so, it is the very catalyst for it. It is the obstacle, the brakes, the guilt, the remorse, the doubt, that tries to weigh you down, thus it lets you find the strength buried inside, the strength you never knew you possessed till Shadow arrived.*

Be grateful to Shadow for the unwilling and unknown support its tireless exertions trigger in you.

Shadow is there to make you long for the Light.

Do not fear it.

Yet do not acknowledge it.

Do not empower it.

Foal had been listening very, very attentively. His mind was buzzing incredulously, as he repeated the words in his head, trying to absorb their full meaning. So, *that* was not the devil, but a part of him . . . of *him?* Really? **Really?** How disgusting! He grimaced. He had never thought he was perfect, but to be so ugly and abhorrent, that was a hard concept to accept. How could he integrate *that* in himself? Such a horrendous, repulsive, frightful being!

And that thought brought him back once again to the big amazement and stupor he had felt when he woke up. How was it possible that he had not been afraid? How could he have possibly uttered those words? And most of all, there was the burning question—Was he ready? How could he be sure of that? And ready for what, exactly?

God Supreme responded promptly and very matter-of-factly:

This doubtful thinking seems to be quite a pattern with you, Foal. Your Soul answered for you. Your Soul is telling you that you are ready for the next level, the next step, the **next you.** *Such a deep unconscious answer is the true answer that only Spirit can give. Your Soul knows better than you do how advanced your evolutionary state is. Good job, Foal, it is quite an accomplishment.* **Accept.**

Foal felt a flood of emotions erupt within him. God Supreme had never been so complimentary before. He felt humbled and overjoyed at the same time. Yet, it occurred to him that he was being so lavishly praised for something he was not even actually conscious of doing. He wasn't even sure that he had said those things! Gosh! It felt so close to cheating! Nevertheless, he thought, God Supreme would obviously already know about this.

God Supreme knew all about him. **"Accept,"** he had said. "All right." conceded Foal, "Why not accept the praises while you can? There may not be many more coming. Who knows?"

∾

Morning found Foal still musing on how, in his dreams, he was always so much more powerful than he was when he was awake. He wondered why this was so and how it was so. Anyway, he really had no answer to that and, well, perhaps it didn't matter after all. Maybe that was his true self, although it certainly felt like there was a huge gap between the dream him and the awake him.

However, he decided to trust God Supreme's words, that his Soul knew better than he did, and, for the moment, he would leave it at that. Yet how wonderful all this was! He was grateful and so overwhelmed by the enormity of it all. The dreams, the messages, the voices. It was becoming a true addiction, he realized, this great anticipation he had every morning when he woke up. Would it ever come to an end? What would he do if that happened? How could he go on without the delight of these voices speaking softly and powerfully in his head?

It was an unsettling thought and he didn't like to dwell too much on it. In the end, he opted for not thinking about it any longer, so as not to spoil the beautiful moments. What comes, comes, he concluded; there was nothing he could do about it, except of course, to enjoy for now.

∾

That evening, as he was still deep in thought, a big Voice filled his head without any warning.

So, how is your heart?

Healing? Expanding? Believing? Trusting finally?

Oh, this was a far better start than Foal could have hoped for.

When we meet again in Light form, you will be surprised at how long it took you, Foal.

I, Metatron, say: How long in life will it take you to realize the greatness of your Being and the Energy you have at your disposal?

Go through the Times of Shift.

Pass into them and out of them as in a cloud.

Be aware of the great potentials.

I AM Metatron and you know me.

Knowing someone has a meaning of faith in itself.

Knowing inside is the very essence of faith.

Know yourself and so know the other.

Knowing the other is an act of faith.

Inspiration comes from the Source.

When it flows, nothing can stop it.

If it stops, do not resist it.

There is a greater scheme in all this, a truly wider plan and you are being given a choice to have a more responsible part in it. **If you cannot find yourself in a greater scheme, you will be lost in your little one.**

The emphasis put on this last statement was so pronounced that Foal's antennae instantly shot up and he found himself riveted to every word.

The great angel went on:

In the way of processing from one spot to one spot, you will notice a difference.

A tiny ripple that makes the difference.

Pick the ripple up.

The ripple of understanding, the explosion of understanding.

In the infinitesimal explosion of understanding, you will find truth.

See through the complex in the simplest way.

In the simplest way all was formed.

And just like that Metatron was gone.

Foal was once more left on his own, puzzling about how mystifying and cryptic Metatron's words could always be. Foal had been listening with total focus, trying to make sense out of what he was hearing, but that was no easy task. It was truly, truly a riddle to him. "How do I pick up a ripple? And *what* ripple?"

Yet, he had this strange feeling; it was like he couldn't understand but he could understand. He knew that it would take time before this subtle subconscious understanding would come up to the surface of his consciousness. He still could not put it into orderly thoughts, let alone words. Nevertheless, despite the fact that at one level it was totally incomprehensible to him, on another, it did feel so incredibly logical and understandable. And how could he explain this? He could only hope that time would bring wisdom and more conscious understanding, so he would be able to be more fully aware of the truth of all these mysterious insights that were being imparted to him.

When night arrived, Foal found himself in yet another dream, not as the player, but as the spectator. This dream proved to be particularly difficult for him to understand, or rather, difficult for him to accept.

⌒ The Souls' Race ⌒

From above, Foal could see the sea and a large sandy beach. A race was going on. People were all racing on the sand toward the same goal, but in an odd way. They were not starting all together, and in addition to that, each of them had to do some different steps and chores on the way to the goal.

Some of them had to pick up something with their mouth; others held a huge heavy package with both hands on their belly, while still others had their hands free and no burden at all. A few were holding strangely shaped objects and doing strange things that Foal didn't fully understand. Some others seemed to be bound together at the leg so they had to run in pairs, and some had to pick up something from the ground on the way to the finish line. But then some guys were running unencumbered and didn't have to play any strange games.

Foal was baffled. It looked so unfair. The most amazing thing to him was that they were not even all starting at the same time. On top of that, a few looked like they started several yards ahead, and others began a few yards behind the starting line. Foal couldn't understand the rules of this race. What kind of game was this? Was nobody there setting any decent rules?

⌒

Foal woke up bewildered and utterly incredulous. He knew what he had seen and understood what he had been shown, but he just could not accept it. It represented a concept staggering to his mind and he felt himself rebelling against it.

"God! It is so **unfair!**" he exclaimed.

Suddenly a big Voice shook him up.

Hmm, did you call me? God Supreme interjected. And as Foal's flabbergasted face flushed with embarrassment and surprise, God Supreme very smoothly and playfully continued. *Oh! I see. Perhaps you called me . . . in vain?* Another big chuckle followed.

Foal felt relieved at the chuckle and a bit offended at the same time. Was God Supreme making fun of him?

God Supreme went on. *Call me whenever you want, Foal. Call me in good faith, though. Call me in good will. So what is all the fuss about?*

Foal spluttered syllables out in a chaotic rush, almost choking on his words. "But . . . but. . . it is so unfair, God Supreme! So **u-n-f-a-i-r**! What kind of race is that?"

Oh, I see. The Souls' Race upset you. One of the most beautiful concepts in the whole universe.

Foal was struck speechless, stared into the air uncomprehendingly. "How can **that** be beautiful?" he barely articulated. And then, picking up some fire, he said, "It is full of cheating and trickery from the very beginning. The starting line itself is not even the same for everyone. And why were there guys with no weights at all, while others had bound legs, had to hold sacks with both arms, or had to start some 20 yards behind? What could possibly be fair or beautiful in that?"

⌒ God Supreme ⌒

Foal, do not give yourself into judgment.

All is not what you see. But of course, you cannot see **All**.

You cannot see how hard it was and how long it took for the man running in front to get to that place.

As I keep telling you, it is about all the decisions, actions, successes and mistakes. That is to say, it is all about the choices you make in all your lives that brings you up to that starting line.

And this is only a very "linear" and summarized explanation for your benefit. It's a way to make you see, so to speak, what you cannot see.

You are the most complete Being in the world, Foal, whatever phase in your Life you go through.

You are made to rebound.

You are made to evolve.

You are made to never get out of the race.

Because you Are the race, and you Are the evolution.

And you Are the seed of creation.

It is all perfect as it is, and if not the body-mind, the Soul does know.

Each of you has the choice to do whatever you like with your life.

That is my gift to you.

But . . . but your next life's hurdles arise from the former one.

It was my gift to you to let you choose your own path with your own will and travel it at your own pace.

No rush. There is not one speck of dust that will not eventually come back to Me.

There are the fast runners and there are the slow runners, but all are running for Me.

∿

A few seconds passed. Foal was completely overcome. Despite his best efforts at trying to take in what he was hearing, he was still in an incredulous daze. His thoughts were unmanageable. He still could not see, still thought it was the most unfair thing he had witnessed, and still thought those poor guys did not deserve such treatment.

It was maddening and disconcerting at the same time, and he badly needed some more explanation, but he didn't feel like making objections to God Supreme again. Just as he was wondering what to do, he felt another great Presence. He recognized it at once.

"Lord Michael, is it you? Please, please help me understand, because I can't! It is so unfair! They don't deserve this!"

The reverberating voice was suddenly all over his head.

⌒ Lord Michael ⌒

F*oal, it is not about what you deserve or do not deserve. God doesn't judge you by what you deserve. Actually, he doesn't judge you at all.*

Divine Logic has no such standard and oversees all.

Divine Guidance will lead you as you let go of old paradigms that are still holding you back. Let them go.

Do not compare yourself to others and do not judge the others' Path. Each has a different Path.

Trust in a greater Will, and be thankful for all that is being given to you, because it may be taken.

*"Enjoy" the present as you have it, which actually means **"bring joy"** into your present and give thanks to God that you have it.*

Think not of deserving in human terms, but what "Deserve" is in God's Eye.

You shall deserve the joy you make, and you shall take merit for the happiness you build.

This was said in such a compelling way that Foal's mind was completely blown away.

And after a few breaths, Lord Michael continued:

It is not unfair, Foal, as there is no fair or unfair. There just IS.

Now, as you are entering the country of your Soul, the crags and rocks, the unseen valley, the forests and the mountains, go for the treasure.

*Without searching, **go for the treasure.***
*Without looking for it, **go for the treasure.***
*Without expecting, **go for the treasure.***
It is each step as each moment of Now that will take you there, and when you least expect it, you shall see it.
*As I said, it is not "deserved." It is **given** and it is **bestowed** upon him who seeks in purity and with no expectations.*
Do not expect reward for finding the treasure.
The treasure is not deserved and is not rewarded.
The treasure IS.
The meaning of deserving is human-made; the meaning of reward is earth-bound.
When you get there, you will have transcended the concept of reward; you will be beyond the concept of merit.
You will feel the perfection and the ease and the peace.
*Love is the ultimate perfection of **you**.*
*Lacking nothing, exceeding nothing . . . perfect in its **Being**.*

And he was gone.

"Wow, that was long," thought Foal, "and that was **amazing**!" He realized he had to change his perception of all things, and, although he was still struggling to regain his mind composure, he felt somehow soothed, and little by little, his feelings started to clear up.

Disbelief unexpectedly vanished and it felt like understanding was slowly, quietly, very quietly taking its place. His mind went over the images of the dream in a more objective way. He tried to remember all the teachings he had received since the first angel.

He grabbed a pen and jotted down his unraveling thoughts in haste, hoping to make the clouds of confusion clear his mind's sky. And so he penned a few random lines:

*To the human me, looked very unfair, but from
Divine Order's perspective, must be exactly how
it is supposed to be. Even if we can't understand
humanly . . . each of us has a different destiny
to fulfill, different processes of learning in our
Evolution Race. Some light, some heavy. So the
seeming unfairness must stem from our past lives
and our past achievements and our learned or
unlearned lessons.*

*Our starting line is probably different according to
what we deserve or do not. Oops, no, deserve is not
the right word it seems.* <u>*Okay then, our starting line
is probably different depending on what we are in it
to learn, so that we grow spiritually.*</u> *I can't really
explain the feeling I have, but it feels clear to me
now in a "knowing" way, not a rational or logical
way. It makes a strange kind of sense.*

Foal put down his pen with a pensive look. Was he
getting it all right, was he keeping up with their teachings?

God Supreme surprised him by speaking out of
nowhere again. The Voice felt soft-spoken this time, as if
He desired to finish His explanation.

*Foal, you are doing well. Do not blame the limitations of
your mind, but understand with your heart.*

*From a combination of various events, you are what you
are now.*

As you were the many things you were before.

But there is a thread in all of them.

*You change dress, you change personality, but you, "the
Seeker," remain the same.*

The Seeker. Let the Seeker seek.

And let the Seeker find.

How many Beings are contained in one little spot in your Soul! And they all make you, and they all have Me inside. When you find Me inside of you, you will be out of the race.

I AM that I AM
I AM

And I surge in you with every life you beget of your wishes and whatever flesh you choose to wear.

I AM who you are
I AM that I AM

So be it and so it is.

~

Foal tried to take all that in. On the one hand, he felt much closer to true understanding, but on the other, he still had so many questions. One felt more pressing than the others. It was burning him up, actually, but for some reason, he couldn't bring himself to formulate it. Not now, not yet. But he knew that the day would come when he would feel compelled to ask.

Maybe he needed some more time to choose the right words, maybe he wasn't ready, maybe. . . maybe what? "Okay, I'll sleep on it," he thought. "I can always stack it up on my collection of endless issues and inquiries." And as he was slowly falling into a deep sleep vowing to himself to make sure to find the courage and ask, a Voice coming from everywhere and nowhere murmured:

Whenever you like, Foal. Whenever you feel ready.

~

However, the next night, the Archangel Chamuel came in with such amazingly beautiful and wondrous words that any doubts or questions he may have been harboring were totally forgotten.

ᐧ Archangel Chamuel ᐧ

Sharing your Light, Foal.

What humans are supposed to do on Earth, share their Light. And make it **One**. With such great resonance that all the universe will be witness to it.

Share your Light with the small and the big, the good and the bad, the base and the lofty.

Share your Light.

Humans are mostly concerned with talking of sharing, but rarely do they truly share. You still don't see that Light is information and brings information. In sharing Light, you will be sharing information with all.

You all miss the point in trying to control.

You can never control the Light of another, yet you can share it.

Foal listened, spellbound. The Archangel pronounced these last words with such ineffable beauty, Foal felt instantly and totally entranced. The great angel continued:

God's Breath is Light.

When Light was infused into your cells, you came to be. The spark of Life into the cells is Light. Light is part of your Soul.

Little brains think themselves big. But the real Source is not in the brain. The real Source is the Light you hold inside.

The Light you emanate in every action, in every word, in every thought you generate.

Talk to me in the great silence of your Soul.
Where I come from, you come from.
It is the Source, the very beginning, the very end.
It is the Soul of the universe.
It gives life to All.
It is the wind of the universe.
It gives power as energy to All.

Each little rock, meteor, comet.
All are pulsating with Life.
The Breath of the universe pulsating into it.
The Prana of the Soul, the Prana of Spirit is in every-
thing, **everywhere.**

The Life you have in you is part of the Life of All.
It is yours, but not only yours.
It is yours, but it is shared by All.

I am a field of energy and I have always been around.
I have known you forever and you know who I AM.

Foal was mesmerized. He had never imagined Light in such a way. So Light is living stuff, he considered. And everything is made of Light, even rocks, meteors, and comets. So everything is alive. Alive and made of the Light of God. Which means that everything must have intelligence, then . . . Wow! It was astounding, astonishing, and yet, why did it make so much sense?

The angel's words resonated inside of him with such truth that he lost track of all rational thought. And then, most unexpectedly, as he had just started to set his thoughts in order, again there was this big rushing in his mind. He was surprised. What was it? It felt as if it was a new energy coming through, but, two in a row? That had never happened before. Without any preamble, the Voice spoke.

⤙ Archangel Gabriel ⤚

F oal, this is Archangel Gabriel.
Voice of music and high frequencies do I have.

There are colors in the frequencies of sounds. So we spin in those colors and our energy manifests in them. Like a rainbow of lights dashing through the universe. Like a brilliant comet made of all colors.

And there is a great symphony of sounds in you too. Mathematics and music and colors are already in the body. They are correlated, because each sound **is** a number and **is** a color. At a minuscule scale, sounds have a different quality. Thus cells vibrate in different ways so that they can recognize each other.

Messages in the form of sound and light are brought about the physical vessel by water. Water is the carrier of sound and light, because water absorbs light, therefore information, and brings it everywhere it has to.

Light gave Life to life. See how photons move around DNA. The symphony of the cosmos is outside and inside, and there is a close relationship between them.

So Light became Sound.

So the **Word was**.

The **first sound was**.

The **first vibration** shook the worlds alive.

Sound can bypass "boundaries" of dimensions, Foal. Sound is sacred as the Sound of Creation is. **The sounds are the way to the heart.**

Be extremely careful, though. Sound can be a two-edged sword. Do not use sound lightly. Find the right sound-wave to communicate.

So many waves, waves as sound, as vibrations, as frequencies, and the waves of Light. Through different dimensional waves the universe is in contact with you, and you, potentially, with the universe.

I always bring Love.

I AM a messenger of Love.

So be it and so it is.

∾

Foal's mind was spinning. "Oh my," he thought, "it is getting confusing again." These ideas seemed so farfetched, almost inadmissible to his tiny mind. "Each sound is a number and is a color," "the mathematics of the notes," "photons," "DNA"? He was disconcerted, mystified, perplexed, bewildered, and totally confounded.

What he had just heard was utterly mysterious to him. Yet what could he say to that? He felt some strange sort of fear rushing up inside him. He squirmed uncomfortably, feeling really small. Small, inadequate, and somewhat afraid. He had hardly acknowledged this thought in his mind when the big Voice of Archangel Michael rumbled in.

⮞ Lord Michael ⮜

L et me tell you what you are afraid of, Foal. Now that you are starting to understand, you are afraid of that very understanding. **What you fear is the Awakening of your Soul.**

This message came in so strong, it felt almost like a physical blow!

The Knowing inside that your world as you know it will cease to exist, will vanish and disappear. The Knowing inside that all you thought true and safe may have to be revalued and reconsidered.

As the Call compels you to make choices you would not have otherwise made. That is what you fear.

Fear of God is not fear of the anger of God.
It is fear of the Love of God.

Once you are touched by Love so great, your life will be turned upside down. When you feel a Love so profound, your Soul will not stay dormant inside you. It awakens and starts capsizing all the values you mistakenly held dear in your life. That is what you are afraid of.

Yet, the Soul awakens in joy—exuberant, ardent, passionate, and compelled by the Calling. All is no more the same. So when you withdraw from God, it is not His wrath you fear, but the very Love He bears you.

Once you see the shadow of God, you can never turn back.

Foal was once again wordless, struck dumb with the shock of recognition, of deep realization. He felt completely out of his comfort zone. He knew how true that was.

∼

He went to bed that night, feeling somewhat rebuked and overwhelmed with some sort of sadness. He was at a loss for words, for thoughts, for everything. He didn't know what to do. How could he cope with this kind of fear? How could he overcome such a subtle intrinsic fear?

With such thoughts in his mind, he tumbled into sleep. Two dreams in a row found their way to him, one more astonishing than the other. They both took his breath away.

☞ The Stag Dream ☜

Foal sees a golden ring rolling on the carpet, as if it were moving of its own will, out of his room and onto the staircase landing. Looking more closely, he realizes that a little whitish spider is pushing it, rolling it over and over on the carpet with great purpose. It is so cute, so tiny, but so determined and full of purpose. He is surprised at the strength it must have to do this. He goes closer to take a better look, but to his utmost surprise, the most beautiful stag is standing in the middle of the landing.

The stag is really big and majestic; it walks around with such a powerful stride that Foal feels awed and overwhelmed, and yes, definitely apprehensive too. So he decides to hide in the nearest room, but just as he is about to close the door behind him, the stag swiftly runs after him and puts his head inside. He actually opens the door with his muzzle, one little push at a time.

It's such a magnificent animal, exuding power from every pore. Foal stands transfixed, looking at him, stunned by such pure beauty. Carefully, he slowly reaches out and touches him on the back. His color is a fawn brown, and the coat hair is short and feels soft and well groomed, which seems strange to him since it is an animal of the wild.

Then he notices its horns. They are special. They are maybe 15 to 20 inches long, thick and powerful, and they sweep backward in a beautiful arch over his neck. But what is so bewilderingly special about them is that they are all painted. It looks like a natural paint, in beautiful soft pastels. Soft blue and soft pink and yellow, all blended and marbled into beautiful arabesques. He is astonished and stays motionless, transfixed with awe, simply gazing and staring at the beauty of it, perceiving the Divinity inside.

Then the scene skips and Foal is now in the middle of the landing where he sees another deer, much smaller and with no horns. He realizes it is a female and she looks startled and is wildly jerking around. She looks so scared that to make her calm down, he covers her head with a dark cloth. As she gradually becomes more tranquil, these words form in his mind: "I wonder whether sometimes it is easier not to see to keep our quiet."

And with these words on his mental lips, he woke up. As his groggy mind tried to make sense of what he had just witnessed, Foal was aware of a strong sense of ceremony in the dream. Starting with the little weaver, symbolized by the tiny whitish spider carrying a gold ring; then the male figure with a painted headdress made up of the horns; and then the female with her head covered by a veil, the dark cloth. The whole dream spoke of a Sacred Union. But the female had been scared and was resisting and had to be blinded.

As he fell asleep again, his last drowsy thought was "the female was me." And then, feeling his mind going blank and unconscious, he was again absorbed and engulfed into one more absolutely stunning dream.

The Golden Cobra Dream

Foal sees himself in a room sitting at a wooden table with other people. This huge serpent, which is as big as the biggest Anaconda he could ever imagine, at least 30 yards long, is coming at him again and again, as if it has a special interest in him. The snake is yellowish brown, with some faint black stripes.

Although it doesn't look as if it wants to hurt him, Foal feels scared and closes his eyes so as not to see. It is so big! Just the head is bigger than two soccer balls put together. As the snake approaches again from behind, Foal feels the big head resting on his right shoulder, just under his cheek. Foal can feel its bifurcated tongue, darting in and out and touching his skin on his cheek and neck. Somebody, somewhere, is saying "It's all right," but he is petrified with fear.

Then the scene skips and he sees himself outside, running on a big dirt trail. He is on the left side, running like mad, and the huge snake is pursuing him a few yards back in the middle of the path. Then, all of a sudden, for some unfathomable reason, Foal just feels compelled to stop and look back.

His heart skips a beat. What he sees takes his breath away! He has never, ever seen anything more beautiful! The huge serpent is in the middle of the path and it is all gold, huge and **gold**! It is all gold, pure shining gold! Its cheeks are now all puffed up, rather like a cobra, and they are reflecting the bright gold rays of the sunshine.

From the nose to the puffed-up cheeks there are some dark cobalt stripes, which remind him of the golden mask of Tutankhamen. The serpent is looking right at him, or rather, right into him. His eyes seem to bore holes into Foal's. Foal cannot take his eyes off the snake. He stands transfixed and he has stopped running.

He can see everything, up to the smallest details. He can see the golden muscles rippling under the surface, so strong and supple in their swift bending movement, yet made of solid gold and reflecting the sunlight. He can see the golden hood completely raised and inflated, the eyes exuding and impressing sacredness. The serpent towers over Foal in all his majesty.

A King Cobra. A God Cobra. Like one of those ancient Gods. So incredibly beautiful, so sacred.

Foal woke up in an ineffable and liberating stupor. A flood of understanding overwhelmed his mind. He needed to make sure all was down on paper, in case he forgot, so he grabbed his pen and started to write it all down in a rushed fury. This is what he wrote:

I think it's the same theme as for the Stag dream.
I am fascinated by the Divine, but I feel so small,
awed and overwhelmed by it. After reaching out, I
always try to run away, but It comes after me until
I am forced to look at It, to acknowledge It. I feel
scared of such beauty; I feel that I am not yet ready
to look directly into so much Living Light. But the
Divine is not one to let us go easily and it comes

*after us and begs us to look at It. **Relentlessly.** And as we stop to look, we discover all the beauty and Love that has been there all along.*

Then, after a few seconds, he added:

Still, I needed a cloth over my eyes to approach such Divine Beauty, not to be blinded by such Light. I needed to be blinded to keep calm. I think the two dreams are telling me I need to stop hiding away and fearing the Divine Power I have inside. They are telling me to take full control of all the gifts that have been bestowed.

After writing these few notes down, Foal was somewhat happy with himself, feeling that he had finally identified the kind of fear that held him back, hidden deep inside. At the same time, he was not sure he could make the fear disappear, and that troubled him. As he was deep in his worries, he felt some soft change in the air of his mind, so gentle, so warm, so all-pervading . . .

"Oh! This is a feminine energy," he thought. He felt excitement rise up within him. **Yes!** He really needed a mother-like figure in this moment, some suave soft energy to soothe his fears and doubts! And certainly a Mother he got. She introduced herself as the Divine Mother, the Mother of All.

⤔ Divine Mother ⤕

Words of truth for those who look for them.
In spite of all the sufferings in the world, there is joy and Love in every heart. In sorrow and grief there is joy hidden still, if you can see its infinity. To bring it out in times of dire need is the mission and message of the Masters.

It is the message of the child, the child in you. Bring it out, let it play and fly at will, let it bring joy and Love to you and those around you. This is the way of the Inner Child in you.

Let it be ego-free. Ego is just another energy to be transformed. Ego is energy given to you to elevate your potentials. It was always meant as a tool, not a way of being; just as the tool itself was never meant to get bigger than the bearer.

I leave it to you to forge the tool, so that **you** can use **it**, not **it you**.

Allow space for Spirit to be.

Foal, **turn your ego into compassion.**

The compassion in you is an ancient flower. It bloomed also in the greatest darkness, and it became your sun of Light in the dark night of the Soul.

So, do you remember me and recognize me as your eternal friend?

You started losing fear of your demons when you felt compassion for them. Wherever you go, there will always be dragons to be found. Wherever you search in your heart, you will find the shadow of them lurking to envelop you in doubt.

You are trembling in the heart for reasons quite incredible to believe. Be open to the potential of the miracle that is going to appear at your doorstep. Mold your fear to your very self; become one with it and then release it. Discharge it from your being, after acknowledging it as yours. Drop it and send it on its way.

Let the gates of your heart open. Let the great miracle happen, let it fill your heart with joy, for few are so blessed.

What is it you are trying to resist so forcefully? You fear the bringer of joy, you fear your horizon expanding, you fear what will make your Bliss, you fear this, but how come you don't fear the lack of Love in the world?

Be yourself. Be your strong fearless self. Fulfill who you are and what you came to do. It is fulfillment you seek now. It is fulfillment you long to reach.

After a few seconds of quiet, the Divine Mother went on:

Like the birds in the sky,
Like the fish in the water,
Shall you be.
Like flowers in the meadow,
And trees on a mountain slope,
Shall you be.
Like the air filling the sky,
Like the water flowing in the streams,
Shall you be.
Where freedom of the Soul and wisdom of the heart can be found in Spirit.

If you love as you have always loved, it will not be enough. *Not anymore. You will feel the need to be surrounded by it in every moment of your being.*

In Love you can ask anything
In Love you can receive anything.

~

And she was gone.

Foal shook his head in amazement. The celestial words were still floating in the air. He was totally enthralled with their beauty and awestruck by the grandeur of her Presence. As time progressed, he became lost in the soft aura she left behind and, all the while, he held on to this sense of peace and Love and stillness inside; he silently and serenely drifted into his own sleepy reveries.

That is why he was more than surprised when in the very early hours of the morning, he was sent such an uncanny dream. He actually remembered very little of the story itself, but the last scene was etched in his mind, as if it had been left behind on purpose, hovering in his memory.

⌁ The Stick Dream ⌁

A big white-haired man with a beard is standing with his back leaning on a fence, his arms crossed in front of his chest. The man looks quietly up at Foal, deep into his eyes and says, *You must stop using the stick (to walk).*

The last words "to walk" were not pronounced out loud, actually, but were kind of implicitly transmitted. Foal didn't know why, but he intrinsically and absolutely knew the big white-haired man was God Supreme.

Foal woke up bewildered. God Supreme had been there in his dream and had taken the form of an old man just to tell him to stop walking with a stick? Fancy that.

What is there to fancy about? God Supreme silently boomed in.

Foal couldn't help himself, and he blurted out without thinking: "You came into my dream just to tell me that?"

Hmm . . . just to tell you that . . . God Supreme retorted. ***"That" is the story of your life, Foal!***

Foal almost gasped. A few moments passed in silence. He was stung, hurt. In truth, he felt devastated. Shame spread within him. He knew exactly what he was being told. He knew that the depth and the implications of the meaning greatly surpassed the surface of the simple words. Just as he knew that he felt it so strongly, because the blow hit super-home, right into his heart. God Supreme plodded on.

☞ God Supreme ☜

A ctually it is the story of almost all human lives. The living with the excuse, with the "well-thought-reason-for"
ready under the sleeve for just anything you want to do or you
want to avoid.

Walking with a stick is avoiding being responsible. What
is a stick but the illusion, the delusion, all the forms you form
to help you walk erect, while you are already erect as you were
made. The stick helps you avoid assuming responsibilities.
Don't skirt your responsibility. When you are responsible, you
are in the moment, you are **living the moment** and you are
ready to take your life fully onto yourself.

**Using a stick is only indicative of your disability to
respond.**

Walk straight, erect, fully Present each step of the way.
Be responsible for your choice.

Foal, his head on his chest, not knowing what to say,
murmured something unintelligible under his breath.
God Supreme continued more softly.

And as for—what word did you use before?—the "form"
I chose? Right . . . quite a popular image, isn't it?

Ooh! You didn't like it! Don't humans love to depict me
in such way?

Foal barely registered the usual chuckle, and,
although hearing it eased his mind somewhat, he could
hardly bring himself to smile. "The story of my life, the

story of my life . . . How pitiable, pathetic." . . . Yes, he knew he had always had a stick ready to use somewhere close to him. Random images and scenes of his life started flipping chaotically in his head.

You see, Foal was not an irresponsible person, but he knew that to stay in his comfort zone, there were times when he had not gotten as involved as he could have. There were times when he could have helped but hadn't, for fear of getting too involved and losing his free time. There were times when he could have volunteered but hadn't, fearing he might get entangled in social relationships and lose his autonomy. All the many "little" times when, to hold on to his freedom, he had decided to draw back, to hold back, to stay away, rather than get involved.

Foal mumbled, his voice was just a whisper now. "Yes, of course, I see. . . . I tend to do that."

God Supreme boomed on.

What are you whining about, Foal? **Be in your full power.** *Stop feeling sorry for yourself, stop pitying yourself, stop finding excuses for yourself.*

Freedom, you say. Is freedom all you worry about? What do you know about freedom? What is true freedom, Foal? **The choice has the freedom of the Soul.**

Do not be afraid of getting involved in your life; do not be afraid of the possible blunders, or mistakes, or obligations and commitments that may come along with it. Live. Live the Life I gave you. **By accepting Life you will find freedom.**

Accept the responsibility of living your life fully, and you will indeed find freedom inside. Fully, as fully involved in all you do, in all that is happening around you. Interact, include, commit yourself; be responsible for all you are involved with. Life becomes full, and that fullness is no baggage; it is no load to weigh you down.

That "baggage" is full of the gifts I expect you to bring **Home** *to Me. All the gifts of wisdom you have gained by taking on your responsibilities to live life to its full potential. That is the kind of "baggage" I want you to take* **Home** *with you.*

Your responsibilities are the true key to life itself. In life, good things happen and bad things happen. You are responsible for All.

You are responsible for All.

YOU . . . ARE . . . RESPONSIBLE . . . FOR ALL.

Take the **huge** *responsibility to make things happen.*

The power of manifestation is proportionate to the grade of acceptance of responsibilities.

That is the power of fully aware choice.

The Energy of Creation. The Energy of the Creator.

And it is not just a matter of responsibilities to others. What about the responsibilities you have toward yourself, **toward your Soul**? *Go inside, gather yourself and feel the moment of bliss that I give you Now, that I'm giving you Now,* **that I'm always giving you Now.**

That IS the blissful moment of Now.

Could I confiscate your many thoughts, I would. But it is not My call and it is not My choice. *It is your Soul's work to do. So, do it.*

And be with me.

BE with me.

Stop the melodrama and start living. You are a powerful, beautiful Being. Such beauty.

The human race is a creation of such beauty, such power.

Foal timidly, hesitantly, murmured "We are?"

God Supreme thundered back:

Yes! You are! *You are indeed! The Spirit sustaining you is glorious, resplendent, in spite of all the abhorrence committed by Shadow. You are my most beautiful creation.*

I Love you so.

*The beauty of you Foal, the incredible beauty of you. You
are my perfect creation and I Love you **All**.*

Foal could feel that Love enfolding his whole self,
and he soaked it all in and basked in it, yet he could not
help himself from artlessly uttering: "But what do you see
in us? Lord, I don't know what you see in me."

*I see Me in you, I see My creation in you, in All of you.
All the Love I AM is there reflected in you.*

And with this, God Supreme left just as quickly as
He had arrived.

～

Foal felt an incredible surge within. He felt so completely
overcome and wrapped in the love of his God, such cosmic Love. Emotions swelled within him as the rushing
and warmth of Spirit flowed through his veins, his All
self. He basked in the magnitude of what he was expe-
riencing, bathed in the incredible peace that permeated
every cell of his being.

All at once, he felt Light being born inside, a surging of Light from his guts upward, a rushing of Light
expanding from inside of himself outward, forward, like
Light bursts from within pouring forth, out of him, wham,
Wham, **WHAM**, in three steps he felt he was on top
of the Himalayas, then further and further, higher and
higher! There was no limit to him; he was expanding,
expanding and, incredibly and unexpectedly, this feeling
of bliss, oh God! The Bliss! Thoughts vanished, leaving
only vastness and peace. He was immense. Infinitely. His
egg cracked. His bubble burst. His Soul broke free. His
heart seemed to shatter into a million pieces. And each

piece glimmered with the immensity of his being, and each piece was **One**. It was utterly liberating. Foal was in bliss, he was the Bliss, and he forgot where and who he was to such an extent that he almost lost consciousness.

∽

Morning came unexpectedly. "Does morning still come?" wondered Foal. "Does Time still rule the world?" His universe was upside down. He had difficulty recollecting his thoughts. Mmm . . . did he still have thoughts? Nothing was the same anymore; he knew he was profoundly changed in a way he could not process, and yet, . . . still . . .who cared?

He felt himself beaming joy on a happiness cloud surrounded by singing cherubim; he felt all was right in the world and nothing mattered but the peace he had found within. The funniest thing of all was this new sense of poise, of perfection, this balance inside that had always eluded him.

The thought fleetingly occurred to him, and to his total and utter dismay, that he would never be able to get angry again in his life. He even gave it a try, to see what happened, but in his emotional state, there was no way anger could surge in him.

However . . . however. . . , big **however** . . . , the wondrous sense of immensity of the night before was gone. With some sort of wistfulness, he realized his infinity was gone. He recognized deep in his heart that his energy at his present level was not capable of sustaining such a state of grace for long. For him, that was a terrible blow, of course, but he was also acutely aware of the magnitude of what he had received.

It was such a significant and essential moment for Foal. The discriminating cerebral part of his mind had burst its bubble for a tiny moment. It felt as if there was now such new dimension to his life. This "thing" that had happened to him was something he would never forget and it would always stay with him, as some mystical, yet so physical and tangible, experience to make all his doubts disperse. All his doubts and, hopefully, fears too, he prayed.

All the deeply buried Love for God exploded inside him, as intense throbs of longing for the Divine enfolded him; at the same time, a deep euphoria took over his heart. He felt so thankful, so very intensely thankful, his heart swelled with gratitude for this experience that had been granted to him.

As he was lost in his thoughts trying to recall and recapture and relive every single moment of that mystical "something," a sweet, vibrant energy emerged from the peaceful space in his mind.

☞ Angel EM ☜

Hi, Foal, it's me! EM!
In such an ineffable moment, let me share your Light,
let us share your Light so that we become **one bright Light** to
be seen by All and from far above!

Yes, let me share your Light, Foal, as you now shine as
you never have before.

For the future Being you are now and for the past Being
you are now, I here stand in Love and loyalty.

Mmm. . . . So, gratitude. What a wonderful gift to have
a grateful heart. Gratitude awakening you in the morning and
gratitude putting you to sleep at night. Know gratitude and
you know the Path to God. From the first conscious breath of
today to the last. And in the dream state, do not leave your
gratitude behind. Gratitude of the heart brings radiance along
and reflects its luminosity on your very shadow. Ten thousand
and one reasons to have gratitude in your heart.

**Be thankful for the many blessings that you see as
such, and the very many blessings that you do not recognize as such.**

Remember to light the flame of gratitude in your heart.
Pour oil on its flame and see the great shower of gifts pouring on you from above. Gratitude brings more gratitude and
more gratitude. Learn the power of gratitude. Let it happen
in your life.

In an infinite space within you

Light rejoices, joy resides, Life IS.
This is EM, Foal. Let us be one Light.
"Yes, of course, EM!" cried out Foal. "I so want to share my Light with you! I'm not sure how to do it though. Maybe you can come into my heart? You can live there, stay there all you want!"
I am already in your heart, Foal, and you have just turned the Light on!
And the Energy that was EM was gone.

∾

"Ohhh!" breathed Foal. All of a sudden he felt like some huge energy had just landed and stood still there right in front of him. Was this his imagination playing tricks on him? But then, what felt like one big stretched wing covered him as in an embrace, and then, as the other wing came down too, folding over him so sweetly, he started melting inside, so tightly held in such a wondrous clasp, pressed to the angelic bosom. And as he finally gave in to the pure sensation of it and let his head rest in this embrace, the Light was turned on.

He felt a surge of focused intensity inside, like being touched in a little spot by a tiny finger of Light. There was this sense of Light and joy bouncing back and forth within his body. He felt all warm and tingly inside and, and . . . shiny! Yes, shiny! What a groovy feeling! He felt energized by all this shininess and marveled at the sense of enhanced clarity and courage he felt he could now muster.

He immediately perked up and was struck by a sudden inspiration. The thought kept coming up that he should, yes, he should, he should, he really should. . . . And the thought, once it started percolating in his mind, would not give him rest. After all, he felt very keenly about this. It had always been a problem in his life, something he didn't know how to accept or how to cope with.

He thought that this was the one question that possibly even God Supreme might not have right. Yes, it was time to voice his doubts; now it was time to ask the burning question. He studied the air around him, feeling sure that he would be answered, and then he blurted out:

"God Supreme, you are there, right? It's about the Souls' Race again, if I may . . . hmm . . . well, are you there?"

Of course I AM, wherever would I be?

"Yes, sure. I am sorry to be so insistent. You see, about the hurdles, the big challenges, the not-unfairness you mentioned . . . with all due respect of course. . . ."

Come on, Foal, speak right up! Do not hold such hesitation in your heart and say it out loud, right?

Foal once again took his chance. "Okay, then, out loud, yes. How . . . how about the children who die too young, too soon, and leave desperate families behind? Isn't that unfair?"

God Supreme spoke with great deliberation.

God Supreme

Foal, there is no such thing as too young or too soon to be reborn on the Other Side. It is never too young to be reborn. You live here, you live there. That's all.

Who would not rejoice at a celestial birth? You are just awakening from your dream. And you may even get your better part of the bargain there, you know.

Big chuckle.

Okay. See it like this—rather than a passing away or passing on, it is a passing through. From one dimension to another veiled dimension.

Imagine yourself being transferred to another country for a few universal moments—a very, very brief vacation in universal "No-Time." You leave family and friends behind maybe, in that particular frequency shape, but you will be reunited in no time, I mean, really human no time.

What is the big deal?

Rest assured, **you live.**

Nothing can harm you but your own self.

You are indestructible, perfect, Divine.

You are Life.

Life trapped in a limited form, inside an involucrum that permits and gives you access to form. How formidable is that, huh?

No one goes too young or too soon.

It is just energy that moves at a different speed.

~

Foal stood motionless. He was brooding. Hearing what God Supreme said had, yes, somewhat eased his questioning and confused mind, yet, with a studious look printed on his face, he was pensive. He could accept and understand that we get born again there, that we don't die, that Life IS, all of that . . . yet, nevertheless and in spite of all, the pain would still be so great. How do you cope with such pain? So he emphatically blurted out:

"That doesn't help with the pain though!"

God Supreme replied undauntedly,

You are still united at all levels but the physical, Foal. The departed are with you indeed, as they have never left indeed. They do miss you, as much as you miss them, and they surely do care for your well being, **but. But**

Souls have other covenants.

And these are big, long-term, and unstoppable.

All is disposable for a greater end.

This is the soul's perspective.

Souls are not concerned about family or finance or illness. Souls do not take into consideration pain or grief, nor do they squander time over the reason-why for crossing-overs. There could never be a just, appropriate, understandable **reason** *for grieving families.* **The reason for the final commitment of a Soul to finish one cycle and start the next.**

All of you actually know your lifetime limit before you incarnate into physical structures, but if your minds remembered, you could never live, right? Indubitably and most unquestionably, you could never go on living your lives fully if you remembered your final commitment's hour. You would not know how to cope with such knowledge and would not know how to live as if you didn't know.

Foal, abandon judgment.

The parting is a trial and a lesson more for those who remain than for the passing one. There is no logical reason understandable from your parameters. Universal reasons explain themselves in cycles of centuries and millennia of evolutionary lives. A dot in universal time.

It is almost impossible to describe or explain this to a Soul incarnated in a human body. If you think of death as the ultimate tragedy, life is a "tragedy-bound" journey then.

Yet Foal, know this.

If you are free of too many attachments, such as envy, jealousy, resentment, any kind of unfinished business, and you are able to keep your consciousness awake, it will be pure joy for the Spirit inside to soar free of the body . . . liberated, unbound, finally released, at last **free** again!

Ties and lives are multiplied and multiplied again and over again, but this knowledge does not bring consolation to the incarnated Soul living in the lesson, oblivious of the greater reality.

Foal, abandon judgment.

The "Why me?" assumption is again Earth-bound.

You are not Earth-bound.

You cannot be "bound." If there is a "Why me?", there must then also be a "Why the Other?". Actually, there is no "Why" at all. How could you, as an incarnated human, understand reasons for a thousand-fold Life Choice of a Being?

Do not fear the parting of people who are supposed to leave. Do not fret about the untimely "goodbyes." You are getting drained and confused over an illusion. Just give Love to what and who is around you, to the coming ones, to the going ones.

Pain and grief are there for your growth, to help you rise to your potential. To see through that is to see through the Veil, *and that is attained by so few. In truth, it is, indeed, no easy feat. Yet that is the lesson for growth.*

Life and gratitude must not be wasted on grief, only exalted by it.

If you don't infuse grief with Light, if you don't bestow upon it the power for change, grief will end up being overbearing, cluttering, and destructive of growth—not the catalyst it is supposed to be. Use grief as a springboard to fly higher, not to fall down into a precipice.

Foal, abandon judgment.

The moments of blessings are always more than the moments of despair.

*The only true consolation I can give you is that **life is**, that **Love is**, and that is what goes on forever and forever and forever still.*

The Angel of Compassion did speak to you the truest words. I hope you have not already forgotten.

"The bleeding heart sows beautiful seeds in the land.
Its vibration reaches down, density lifts up.
A bleeding heart is not all about suffering.
A bleeding heart bears the Child of Compassion."

There is nothing I can add to that.

~

With this statement, God Supreme evaporated as usual, but his words had penetrated deep within Foal's heart. Not knowing what to say, Foal simply sat in silence, allowing the unfathomable truth to permeate him.

It was a lot to take in. A lot. But it was amazing stuff, wasn't it? Totally outrageous. So, the question for him now was, would he be able, with all this newfound understanding, to still the pain, to live with it in a more companionable way? Would he be able to "bestow upon it the power for change, to infuse it with Light"?

His mind quaked at the thought of such a challenging enterprise. Nevertheless, he was grateful to God Supreme for having imparted to him such incredible knowledge. He wondered whether, in due time, he would be able to rise to the occasion and appreciate this fundamental truth fully.

"Abandon judgment, abandon judgment . . ." he murmured to himself, God Supreme's words still swirling in his mind. "This is definitely over my head," he whimpered, but deep inside, in a spot that was not his head, he suddenly recognized It.

Foal fell silent. His thoughts dropped. Slowly it dawned on him. There was nothing to understand, or to grasp or comprehend. He only had to accept, allow, to let in, to open the door—to let God in.

It was still early in the day, yet curiously, Foal couldn't keep his eyes open. His mind felt in such a deep daze that he gradually but irrevocably became very drowsy. As he slowly drifted to sleep, he could hazily hear a voice whispering from afar, like an echo from the depths of his dozing mind:

Well said, Foal! Very well said! Expect a dream. Consider it a gift . . .

⇐ The "Kiddo" Dream ⇒

Foal was only vaguely aware that he was in a rural, pastoral setting. He was looking down from above at this idyllic, almost bucolic scene. The sky was a sweet blue with a few sparse wisps of clouds and a joyful sun was shining dazzlingly in the middle. It looked like spring. The grass was green and a few verdant trees were scattered here and there.

In the center of what looked like the start of a long dirt trail that was surrounded by a chest-high fence on three sides, there was a very young child. He seemed fairly unsure on his feet, and he was trying to make his first teetering steps forward on what felt like a very, very long path.

Foal knew he was that child. On the outside, leaning on all sides of the fence, were many people—men, women, children—dressed in various types of countryside clothes from another era, maybe the 1930s or '40s, and they were looking down on him benignly and smiling. They looked so happy, serene, and relaxed, and their eyes were full of affection and support.

As he took his first hesitant and faltering steps, they cheered him on with great anticipation and he could clearly hear them saying, very excitedly: "Let's see how the 'kiddo' does!"

And, unmistakably, the feeling he got was that they meant "Let's see how he fares **this time**," like in this life-time, in this new challenge that is being offered to him. These words had such an impact on him. They were said in such a trusting, loving way that he could not describe. A tear fell from his left eye, and ran down his cheek in a trickle. He was moved beyond words by all these people around him, encouraging him on at every step of the way. And he who had thought that he was alone!

All those people had already passed on, he realized. People he had personally known in this life, and people he had not even physically met, people of this genera-tion as well as people of other generations. They were all watching over him, rooting for him, and more than that, they were all relying on him to finish or accomplish what they probably had not.

It felt as if the baton had been passed over to him now; it was his turn to see what he could make of his life in this one specific given lifetime. He was probably not the anchor, he knew, but he could try to make the best of his stretch of relay.

No, he could not let them down. There was too much Love and anticipation in their eyes. It felt like they were counting on him; they looked happy when he made progress and worried yet encouraging when they saw him faltering, wavering.

But there was one figure in the middle of the fence, one who stood out from the rest because of the shine around her and the beaming smile on her face. She looked as if she was in her mid-thirties and she was wearing an old fashioned type of blouse and skirt. Foal just simply, irrefutably, indisputably knew it was his own Mother, although she looked so young and in such vibrant health.

The very instant he made this realization, she flashed him such a dazzling smile that Foal felt as if he was melting inside. She looked so happy; she was glowing from every pore such Light, such consciousness. His mother had passed on several years ago, and he had missed her so much, but seeing her now, like this, made him realize how she had been looking over him all along, and with such love and support. She'd been totally invisible and inaudible to him, yet, she had been there, she was there, she was indeed there!

He didn't recognize any other face in particular, but he was sure that his beloved father, too, and all his grandparents and great grandparents and uncles, aunts, cousins, friends—whoever was connected to him, not only in this life, but also in other lives—were all there, rooting for him from this fence, from beyond this fence . . . from beyond this Veil that, apparently, so subtly separated them. He remembered how God Supreme had told him that they were still united at all levels but the physical, and now he was being shown that.

He woke up in great joy, feeling that his heart had expanded, his horizons had widened, and, most of all, his greatest fear, the fear of his loved ones' death, had been, incredibly, so magically dissolved. Oh, yes! This was such a **gift** indeed! To be able to see them with his own eyes and feel them!

God Supreme had been so very gracious to answer his burning question in such a paradoxically simple, but inarguable way. "Oh, thank you, thank you, **thank you!**" It now felt as if they were all part of one big team—all family, and friends. . . . Indeed, this must be what is called the Soul-family, he thought. It was a most rewarding feeling and an incredible realization.

Foal felt all wrapped up in warmth and affection. He felt cuddled in such Love. He knew, of course, that the path represented his life, and he also knew that each of us have to stand up and walk on our feet, on our own. Nonetheless, Foal was now filled with a sudden and overpowering certainty: There is not one moment in our life that we are alone. They are just hidden from us, as if they're wearing an invisible mantle . . . hmm . . . was that a flash from Harry Potter? He smiled to himself at the funny idea, but the image was incredibly and startlingly clear for him. Anyway, he knew that the whole point was that we just can't see them or hear them, but they are there. **They are!** We are so immeasurably not alone, not alone at all! Actually, one could say there is quite a crowd!

And then, just as he was getting excited at this stunning discovery, as clearly as anything could be, a chorus of voices from deep in his mind began saying

And . . . *All* goes on, *All* still goes on, *with such as us still by your side.*

Invisible and unheard, mostly, but still by your side.

Evolutionary Paths are unfathomable for those in the human lesson.

But we understand the grief at the loss, and if we cannot console with words, we can be near in Spirit.

We can walk by your side in the hardest times.

We can lift your heart up, when you feel disconsolate.

We can part some of the clouds to make you see the sun shine.

And, most of all, we can inspire you, when you need inspiration.

*Foal, the assurance that you are not alone on the Path,
and that you are being constantly watched and loved by the
progressed Souls, is there for us to give and for you to believe.*

And as the voices trailed off in the air, they continued:
*. . . is there for us to give, Foal . . . is there for us to give
. . . is there for us to give . . . so, belieeeve . . .*

Trying to keep his eyes from sweeping the room
around him, Foal furtively squinted sideways, hoping to
catch a form or shape or anything at all, for that matter.
Giving searching sidelong glances, he thought he saw a
tenuously soft light. He stood still, afraid it would vanish.
The Light spoke from the corner of his eye.

And as soon as the Light spoke in such familiar tones,
he knew immediately who it was. He felt such Love pouring out of his heart into hers and flowing out into the
world, into the sky, into the ether, into everybody's Soul.
And so she whispered, before quickly fading away:

As I have never left you, and as I never will . . .

Foal, remember to care.

*Care for all that is there in your life, from the first smile in
the morning to the last smile before falling into sleep.*

Care!

Care for your life with your **Life.**

Make each wonderful moment of your life full of **Life.**

*Make each devastating, overpowering, uncontrollable
moment of your life full of* **Life.**

**And so the overpowering will grant you power, the
uncontrollable will allow control.**

You are not alone, Foal. Remember.

Do not hesitate to call on us.

The door of Spirit is always open.

Epilogue

Like everyone's story, Foal's doesn't end here. With the angels' clarification and God Supreme's loving rebukes and insights, Foal is surprised and bewildered by the next new experience . . . the "out-of-body."

Please join Foal as the series continues at:
www.foalandtheangels.com (website address)
www.facebook.com/FoalAndTheAngels

You can email the author at: info@foalandtheangels.com